ADVENTUROUS
IN
DORSET

Anne-Marie Edwards

COUNTRYSIDE BOOKS
NEWBURY BERKSHIRE

First published 2003

COUNTRYSIDE BOOKS
3 Catherine Road
Newbury, Berkshire

To view our complete range of books,
please visit us at
www.countrysidebooks.co.uk

ISBN 1 85306 784 9

*For my husband Mike, without whose genius
with map and compass this book would never have
been written*

Photographs by Mike Edwards
Designed by Peter Davies, Nautilus Design
Cover illustration by Paul Vale

Typeset by Techniset Typesetters, Newton-le-Willows
Produced through MRM Associates Ltd., Reading
Printed by Woolnough Bookbinding Ltd., Irthlingborough

Contents

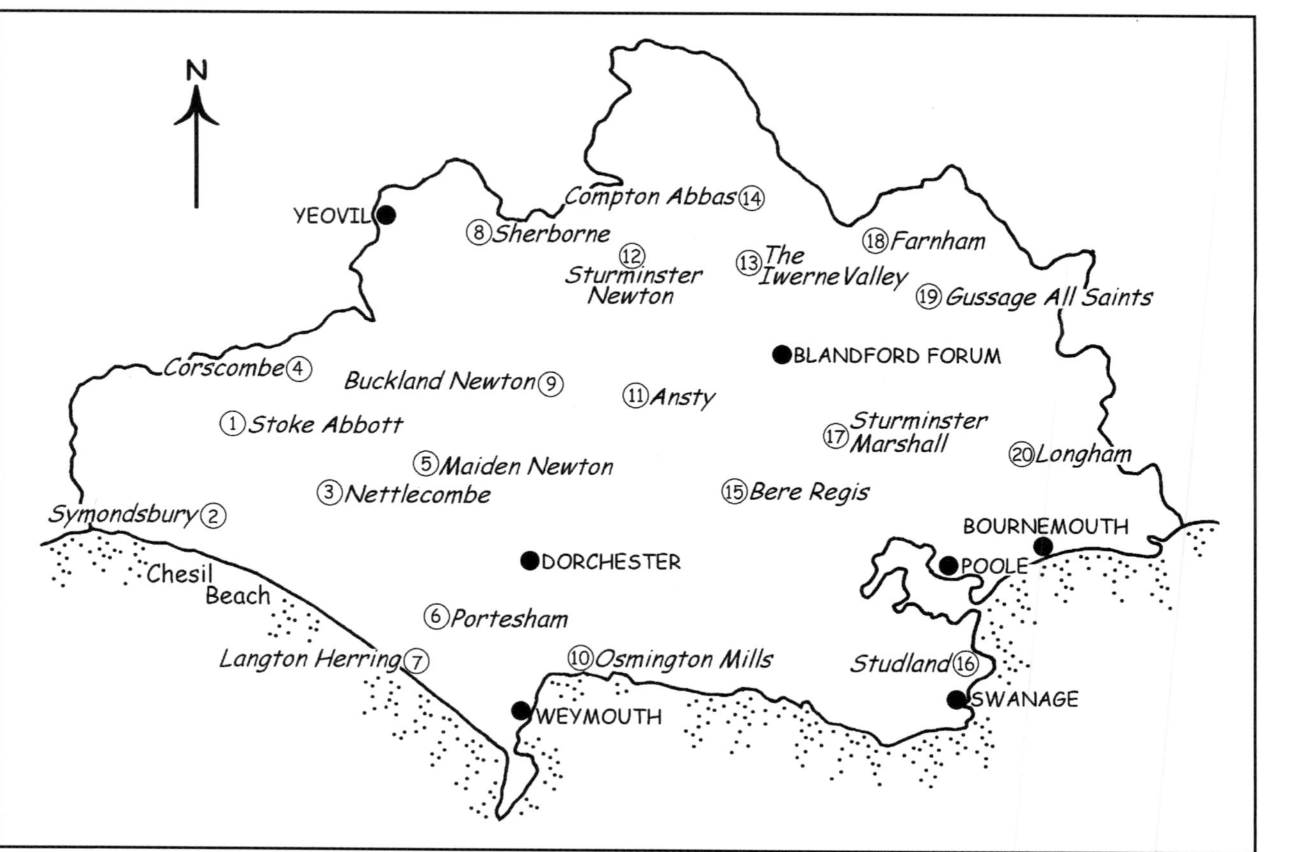

AREA MAP SHOWING THE LOCATION OF THE WALKS

PUBLISHER'S NOTE

We hope that you obtain considerable enjoyment from this book; great care has been taken in its preparation. Although at the time of publication all routes followed public rights of way or permitted paths, diversion orders can be made and permissions withdrawn.

We cannot, of course, be held responsible for such diversion orders and any inaccuracies in the text which result from these or any other changes to the routes nor any damage which might result from walkers trespassing on private property. We are anxious though that all details covering the walks are kept up to date and would therefore welcome information from readers which would be relevant to future editions.

The simple sketch maps that accompany the walks in this book are based on notes made by the author whilst checking out the routes on the ground. They are designed to show you how to reach the start, to point out the main features of the overall circuit and they contain a progression of numbers that relate to the paragraphs of the text.

However, for the benefit of a proper map, we do recommend that you purchase the relevant Ordnance Survey sheet covering your walk. The Ordnance Survey maps are widely available, especially through booksellers and local newsagents.

Introduction

This collection of walks in Dorset is different from any contained in my previous books. They really are adventurous! They were challenging and fun to write and I hope you will find them exciting and enjoyable. They will take you deep into the heart of this lovely county to remote places like the Dorsetshire Gap, a deep cleft in the chalk hills only accessible by a determined walker, and Bracketts Coppice, part of an ancient forest, the tranquil home of deer and badgers, shaded by mighty oaks and beeches and carpeted with wild flowers. Each walk is a journey of discovery and will bring its own sense of satisfaction.

Dorset, with its glorious coastline and gentle rolling hills, is a walker's county. In its many quiet villages tucked away in wooded valleys life still moves at a leisurely pace. There is time in Dorset to stop and chat, to admire a garden, to climb a hill just for the view. The landscape is infinitely varied, often spectacular and specially rewarding if you are prepared to be adventurous and leave the well-trodden ways.

Chalk uplands threaded by clear rivers and streams form the heart of the county rising in the west to Pilsdon Pen, the county's highest hill, ringed, like so many Dorset heights, with the embankments of an Iron Age fort. Nearby Lewesdon Hill retains its ancient beech woods. Further east another Iron Age fort encircles the crest of Eggardon Hill. As you follow the walks you will enjoy magnificent views from these hilltops far over the Marshwood Vale to the coastal downs and the sea.

In the east of the county the rounded slopes of Cranborne Chase were once densely forested. Some of these beautiful woodlands remain – particularly around Ashmore, where you will discover a magical glen.

North of the downs Dorset springs a surprise! Suddenly the chalk escarpment ceases and you look down over the Blackmoor Vale, a world of small, thickly hedged fields, low undulating hills and tiny streams. One of our walks in the Vale visits historic Sherborne, then follows a peaceful valley to Sandford Orcas, an old world village with a Tudor manor house. Another follows the river Stour from Sturminster Newton.

Dorset has more contrasting scenery to enjoy. One ramble leads over the windswept heathland near Bere Regis where Hardy would still recognise his 'Egdon'. Another walk reveals a quite different aspect of this fascinating county as you walk through the lush watermeadows beside the river Frome near Maiden Newton.

Contrast is also a feature of Dorset's celebrated coastline, which provides three exciting walks. The cliffs of Lyme Bay rising to Golden Cap, the highest point on the south coast, give way to the Chesil Beach, a unique bank of pebbles imprisoning the Fleet, England's largest lagoon. The Purbeck peninsula fronts the sea with massive blocks of limestone. East of Purbeck a procession of towering, almost vertical, cliffs leads to the well-known chalk stack of Old Harry.

This tranquil, varied landscape is rich in wildlife. Chalk streams attract kingfishers and dippers, larks soar and sing above the downs. As you follow these walks, venturing into remote areas, the only sounds you will hear are the buzzing of insects in the grass, the rustle of deer in the bracken and the mewing of a buzzard overhead.

The walks are all circular and between 7 and 10 miles in length. Although all the routes follow rights of way – footpaths indicated by a yellow arrow and bridleways indicated with a blue arrow – and at the time of writing are passable, be prepared to tackle stretches that may be overgrown. Dorset specialises in particularly aggressive nettles and brambles so ward them off by wearing long trousers, not shorts. Dorset mud is deep so wear boots, strong shoes or even, after prolonged rain, wellingtons. Often a good path may suddenly vanish at your feet. I have tried to give clear directions at these points and numbered them on the sketch maps, but arm yourself with the relevant OS map noted at the start of each walk.

The pubs I have chosen are as varied as the scenery but all offer a warm welcome, good food and ales and a restful atmosphere. I hope you will find your visits to them as rewarding as I did. Let the management know when you leave your car to start your walk and telephone beforehand if you intend to arrive before opening time.

Finally, I wish you many happy hours following these adventurous walks in this wonderful county, described so aptly by Frederick Treves in his splendid book *Highways and Byways in Dorset* as 'a land of moods and changes that knows no monotony'.

Anne-Marie Edwards

ACKNOWLEDGEMENTS

When writing about Dorset I am always deeply grateful to Edward and Marie Swann, who inspired me with their own love of the county. I am grateful as always to the staff of Totton and Southampton Libraries. In my hunt for books on Dorset I have been ably assisted by Peter Roberts and Georgina Babey of the Nova Foresta bookshop in Ashurst. My thanks also to all the kindly Dorset folk who helped me on my way. As always my publishers have helped me with friendly encouragement and advice, especially my editor, Paula Leigh. Finally, I thank my husband, Mike, my cheerful companion on every step of the way.

Walk 1

STOKE ABBOTT, PILSDON PEN AND LEWESDON HILL

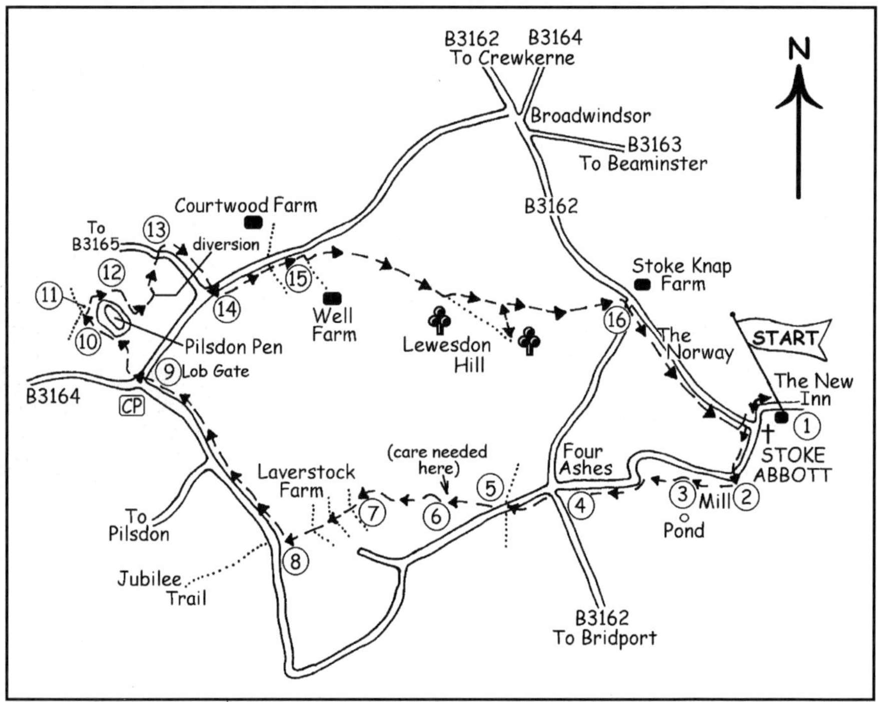

Distance:
7 miles

Starting point:
The New Inn car park. Have a word with the management before leaving your car. GR 454008

Map: OS Explorer 116 (formerly 29) Lyme Regis and Bridport

How to get there: *Stoke Abbott is about 6 miles north of Bridport. Approach via the B3162, the Bridport-Broadwindsor road. Turn for the village and continue for about 3/4 mile to the village street. Head north, follow the street round to the right and the New Inn is on your right.*

THE VIEW OVER THE MARSHWOOD VALE FROM THE TOP OF PILSDON PEN

To walk among the rounded hills of west Dorset is to enter a serene and timeless world. From almost any rise you will be rewarded by wonderful views. To enjoy some of the finest, follow the route of this walk to the top of Pilsdon Pen, at 907 feet the county's highest hill. From the embankments of the Iron Age hill fort ringing its summit you can look south far over the Marshwood Vale and the coastal hills to the sea. North and east stretch the uplands of Wiltshire and Somerset. A ridge path leads on to Lewesdon Hill, beautifully wooded with magnificent beech trees.

We start from Stoke Abbott, an enchanting village of dark-thatched golden stone houses tucked snugly into a hollow at the foot of Waddon Hill.

Stoke Abbott is a kindly village. In the past the villagers had a Sick Club to which everyone contributed a few pence – a real help in times of illness. Each year members met and paraded through the village behind a brass band. After a ceremony in the church there was a dinner followed by sports and dancing. The parade is re-enacted every year in July at the Stoke Abbott Street Fair. To hear all about it call at the splendid village pub, the **New Inn**. Once you have visited this 17th-century thatched pub and enjoyed its warm welcome, delicious food and fine ales you will want to return. Low beamed ceilings, enormous fireplaces and small windows set low in thick walls contribute to its special old world atmosphere. There is a beautiful garden overlooking a wooded valley.

You can relax over a drink or a meal in the comfortable bar area or in the separate non-smoking restaurant. Real ales are Palmers Copper, IPA and 200. A wide range of bar snacks is available and a comprehensive menu. When we called, the 'specials' board included fresh whole grilled sea bass, dressed crab and pan fried duck breast with gooseberry sauce.

Opening times *are from 11.30 am (Sundays 12 noon) to 3 pm and from 6.30 pm to 11 pm. Food is served from 12 noon to 2 pm and from 7 pm to 9 pm. Telephone: 01308 868333.*

The Walk

① Turn left from the pub car park along the road which curves left through the village. You pass two springs, one falling into a trough for animals and the other gushing out of a lion's mouth with a chained iron cup beside it. Cross the foot of a lane that goes to **Broadwindsor**.

This lane is known as the Norway (it runs north) and nearby there is a plot of land called the 'Curfew Plot'. The rent for this is used to pay for the curfew still rung every morning in summer at 7 am!

Just past the lane turn left (signed for the **Village Hall**) to visit the church, which has an elegant 12th-century nave and an exceptionally beautiful font. Retrace your steps to the road and turn left to resume your former heading.

② When the road curves right keep straight ahead along a wide track for about 80yds, then turn right through a gate following the direction of the footpath sign along a grassy track. The first part of our walk follows the Ramblers' **Jubilee**

Trail – look for the sign of a white arrow on a green circle. When the track vanishes keep ahead over the field, leaving a clump of bushes on your left to go over a stile. Cross the next field and another stile and walk downhill to cross double stiles either side of a drive. Bear slightly right down the hill (there is a house and small pond at the foot of the hillside on your left) and go through a gap in the fence on your right.

③ A path leads right over stiles either side of a wooden footbridge and continues ahead for a few yards before bearing left to the foot of a hillside. Walk up the hill, bearing slightly left towards the corner of a hedge, then continue uphill with the hedge on your left. At the top cross the track to **Brimley Farm**, go through a small gate and follow the narrow, thickly hedged path past a house to a lane. Bear left and follow the lane to meet the B3162 at **Four Ashes.**

④ Cross the road and walk up the lane ahead (signed for **Blackney**) for about 200yds to the top of the rise. Pass bridleway signs to left and right. Continue along the lane for another 40yds to a gate on the right and footpath sign.

⑤ Turn right through the gate and keep ahead, hedge on right, to follow the track as it curves left round the edge of the field with a

THE 17TH-CENTURY NEW INN AT STOKE ABBOTT

low fence on the right. The track descends to go through a gap in a hedge. Keep straight on down the next field, keeping a line of power cables a few yards away on your right, to meet the corner of a hedge on the other side. Now for some awkward navigation! Keep straight on with the hedge on your right for only about 200yds, then look **very carefully** for a stile and footpath signs on your right.

⑥ Cross the stile and descend a steep slope, feeling for the steps under the grass. The path drops through woods to cross a plank bridge. Climb the steps ahead and cross a stile. Bear slightly left up the field ahead to go through a gap in the hedge. The right of way continues ahead over the next field but if there is a crop you may prefer to walk round it. If so, bear right and follow a good track as it soon curves left across the top of the field. When you see an iron gate a few yards ahead do not go through it but bear left to walk down the edge of the field for about 200yds to a stile on your right.

⑦ Cross the stile and a farm track and walk down the field ahead, bearing very slightly left. Cross an asphalt lane leading to **Laverstock Farm** and go over a stile. Walk down the field, bearing very slightly right towards a stump with a blue bridleway arrow sign. Continue through a gap in a hedge over a narrow field and go through a gate. Follow a hedged track to a lane.

⑧ Turn right up the lane (leaving the Jubilee Trail) for about $3/4$ mile to meet the B3164 at **Lob Gate** by a parking area on the left.

⑨ Turn left for a few yards, cross the road and climb the stile on your right to take the footpath to the top of **Pilsdon Pen**. There is a board giving details of the hill's history and wildlife by the stile. The path runs to the right of a fence then bears right up steps to wind over the embankments of the hill fort to a trig point by the central plateau. Follow the crest of the left hand embankment to enjoy the wonderful view seawards until the embankment begins to curve right round the north-western edge of the plateau.

⑩ Look for a path leading down the side of the embankment on your left over a dip to a gate by a signpost. Turn left to follow this towards the gate. Turn right just before the gate and follow a narrow path at the foot of an embankment for about 80yds where the path ceases.

⑪ Turn left to a fence then turn right with the fence on your left to walk down to a small wooden gate by a National Trust sign.

⑫ Go through the gate to join the **Wessex Ridgeway**. The path to the foot of the hillside below you has been diverted, so turn right as directed along the top of the hillside until you come to a hedge. Turn left with the hedge on your right to walk down the hill and bear left for a few yards to go through a gate. A broad track now leads to a lane at the foot of the hill.

⑬ Turn right up the lane to meet the B3164 again.

⑭ Turn left to follow the road for a little over 1/4 mile, passing a bridleway sign on the right and the lane to **Courtwood Farm** on your left. Continue beside the road to the next bridleway sign on the right by a shed.

⑮ Turn right for only a few yards then leave the track, which runs downhill to **Well Farm**, and turn left along a bridleway that tunnels beneath the trees to lead you towards the magnificent beech trees on **Lewesdon Hill**. Keep to the left hand track as it runs through the trees with the edge of the edge of the wood 30 or 40yds away on your left. When you come to a National Trust sign you will see a path running uphill on your right. Make a detour here and follow the path to the top of **Lewesdon Hill**, a splendid viewpoint. Retrace your steps and turn right to resume your former heading – east – through the woods. The path leaves the trees to become a sunken stony track leading downhill to meet the B3162 at **Stoke Knap Farm**.

⑯ Turn right then take the lane on the left, **The Norway**, signed for **Stoke Abbott**. This plunges downhill for 3/4 mile to the village street. Turn left to retrace your steps to the **New Inn**.

Date walk completed:

Walk 2

SYMONDSBURY AND THE MONARCH'S WAY

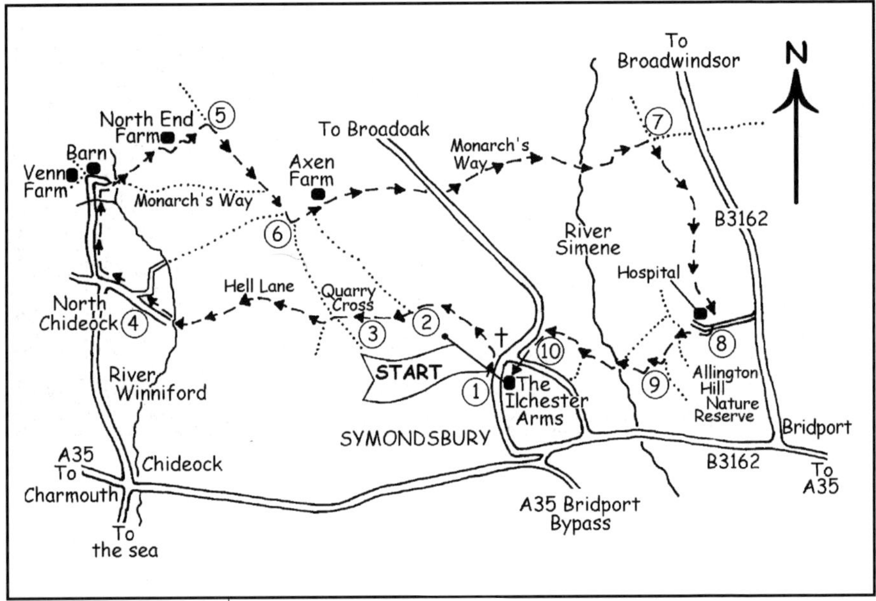

Distance:
8 miles

Starting point:
The Ilchester Arms car park.
GR 445935

Map: OS Explorer 116 (formerly 29) Lyme Regis and Bridport

How to get there: *Symondsbury is 2 miles west of Bridport. The best approach is via the B3162 coming west out of Bridport. Turn right (north) following the sign for Symondsbury, follow the lane round to the left in the village by the church then left again, following the Bridport sign, to the Ilchester Arms, which is on your left. Park in the pub car park or to the left of the road just past the pub.*

LOOKING TOWARDS THE MARSHWOOD VALE FROM QUARRY CROSS

As you travel west in Dorset the countryside closes around you. You find yourself in a self-contained green world of softly rounded hills and wooded valleys. In the past the scattered villages tucked away in the hollows were linked by cobbled roads sunk deep in sandstone gullies. A network of these ancient roads surrounds Symondsbury, nestling at the foot of cone-shaped Colmer's Hill. From the village we climb one of these old roads to enjoy wide views to the sea before descending another ancient trackway to North Chideock. Then we take a path with a more recent history, the Monarch's Way. It follows the route taken by Charles II when fleeing from Cromwell's troops after his defeat at the battle of Worcester. Full details are in Trevor Antill's book *The Monarch's Way*.

After taking a tree-shaded path around Allington Hill Nature Reserve we return along a quiet country lane.

Symondsbury is a gem of a village. All the buildings, including the church, school and larger Georgian houses, are built of locally quarried glowing sandstone in all shades of yellow and gold. Many of the cottages date from the 17th century. We begin this walk from the village pub, the **Ilchester Arms**, which fits the picture perfectly with its overhanging roof of dark thatch and low mullioned windows. It was built around 1325 by order of the Abbots of Cerne, making use of hand-hewn solid oak timbers from the shipyards at West Bay. The timbers supporting the roof in the bar were originally intended to form the keels of ships. Behind a modern grate a huge inglenook fireplace was discovered recently and has now been restored to its former glory. Outside you will find a large streamside garden and a safe children's play area.

There is a separate, comfortable restaurant. On offer is a wide range of appetising dishes. The fish menu is specially tempting, including, when we called, plaice stuffed with prawns and mushrooms. Snacks ranged from ploughman's lunches and omelettes to crispy coated Camembert with raspberry sauce. Real ales include Palmers Copper, IPA and 200.

Opening times *are from 11 am to 2.30 pm and 6.30 pm to 11 pm.*
Food is served from 12 noon to 2 pm and 7 pm to 9 pm. At weekends it is wise to book your meal.
Telephone: 01308 422600.

The Walk

① Turn right from the front porch of the pub and walk up the road past the school. When the road curves right keep straight on up the lane marked by a no-through-road sign. The imposing Georgian building on your left is the former Rectory. It is said to be haunted by a mischievous ghost called Alfred! Continue uphill past a row of very attractive cottages, one of which has a square-arched Tudor doorway with scalloped steps. The lane becomes a track sunk between high banks hung with ferns.

② The track levels to pass a joining track on the right and give fine downland views. On the left the ground rises steeply to the summit of **Colmer's Hill** topped by a lonely stand of pines. The track curves a little left then right between walls of sandstone greened over with moss and draped with ivy. On your right you pass an old gamekeeper's cottage built in the 1600s and said to have been used by smugglers as late as the beginning of the 20th century. Now you continue through a gorge with rock walls over 30ft high in places. The soft surface has been carved with hundreds of initials as well as hearts and faces.

③ Just past a track on the left our way curves right to **Quarry Cross**, where several tracks meet by a finger post. Take the second track on the left, signed (on the reverse of the pointer) for **Hell Lane**. This may sound ominous but 'hell' is probably derived from Saxon 'hele' meaning 'dark'. After about 1/4 mile look over a stile on the right for a delightful view over a lake. Continue down **Hell Lane**, which widens as it approaches the attractive houses of **North Chideock**. The track becomes partly asphalted and then becomes a lane leading gently uphill to a T-junction.

④ Turn left to pass more houses and a lane on the left that goes to **Chideock**. About 100yds further on follow the lane round to the right. The lane dips then rises to face a barn at **Venn Farm**. Follow the lane round to the right, passing the barn on your left. You now come to a gate at the entrance to a Caravan Club Certificated Location. Go through the gate and follow the track beside the site, bearing a little left. Keep to the track across a stream, ignore a bridleway arrow pointing half-right, and follow the track uphill to **North End Farm**. At

THE THATCHED ILCHESTER ARMS IN SYMONDSBURY

the approach to the farm go through a gate and immediately bear right along a track which curves left beside a low wall, avoiding the farm buildings. The track bears right then left uphill to face a wooden chalet. Turn right to walk uphill, hedge on your left. Go through a gate and continue uphill through another gate.

⑤ Turn immediately right along a narrow path tunnelling between high hedges. After about 1/3 mile keep to the same path as the route of the **Monarch's Way** joins us on the right.

We are taking the paths Charles II hurried along after failing to take ship from Charmouth. He intended to spend the night at the George Inn in Bridport. Unfortunately, a detachment of Cromwell's troops were already at the inn; Charles was recognised and narrowly escaped capture.

Continue past the next finger post on the right, signed '**North Chideock**'.

⑥ About 50yds further on navigate carefully! Turn left – there is no sign – to continue along the **Monarch's Way**, which becomes a track leading through a gate past **Axen Farm**. Keep ahead along a good track with splendid views to cross **Broadoak Road**. Go through a gate and follow the grassy, hedged path downhill. When the hedges cease on the left continue with a hedge on the right, following the path through meadows full of wild flowers. After descending to run between trees the path forks. Take the right hand path through a gap in a hedge to a field. Walk straight across the field, aiming for a farm by a thatched barn on the hillside ahead. Cross the gated bridge over the **river Simene** and walk up the hillside with a fence close on your left. Go through a gate, turn left for about 50yds, then turn right through another gate to follow an asphalt track uphill.

⑦ After about 200yds turn right at the footpath sign and continue beside a field with a hedge on your right. Go through a gap in the hedge to cross a stile. Bear half-left then right round the field along a wheel track, keeping a hedge about 30yds away on your left. Keep the hedge on your left as it bears a little left towards a white house then bears right again to bring you to a gate. Go through and keep ahead beside a field, hedge still on your left. Go through a gap in the hedge and continue the same heading with the hedge now on your right. Turn right through the hedge to a good woodland path on your left. Turn left to follow this to a road. The entrance to Bridport Community Hospital is on your right.

⑧ Cross the road and turn right to follow an old cobbled track until it bends sharply right. Turn left into **Allington Hill Nature Reserve** (Woodland Trust) then bear right. After a few yards the path forks. Keep straight ahead (right hand path) through coppiced and mixed woods.

⑨ After about 200yds, when the main path begins to curve left uphill, look carefully for a narrow joining path on the right. Turn right downhill through a metal squeeze gate to leave the wood and enter a field. **NB: There is possibly a dangerous low wire to step over on the edge of the wood.** Turn left to follow the edge of the wood until you come to a gate on the left – about 50yds. Now bear half-right down the field to go through a gateway to a farm track. Turn left for a few yards over the river to a crosstrack. Turn right to follow the track, which curves left past workshops to a T-junction. Turn right again downhill and follow the track as it swings left to meet a road near **Symondsbury**.

⑩ Turn left to follow the road uphill to pass **Symondsbury Manor** and church on your right and the front of the school on your left. Follow the road round to the left (signed for **Bridport**) to return to the **Ilchester Arms** and your car.

Date walk completed:

Walk 3

NETTLECOMBE, POWERSTOCK COMMON AND EGGARDON HILL

LOOKING NORTH OVER THE BLACKMOOR VALE FROM EGGARDON HILL

Distance:
$9\frac{1}{2}$ miles

Starting point:
The inn car park. GR 517957

Map: OS Explorer 117 Cerne Abbas and Bere Regis

How to get there: *Nettlecombe is about $4\frac{1}{2}$ miles north-east of Bridport. Turn off the A3066 Bridport-Beaminster road about $1\frac{1}{2}$ miles north of Bridport, following the sign for Loders. At the junction bear left past Mangerton Mill, drive through West Milton and continue for a further mile and drive straight across a junction. The Marquis of Lorne inn is about 300 yards further on your left.*

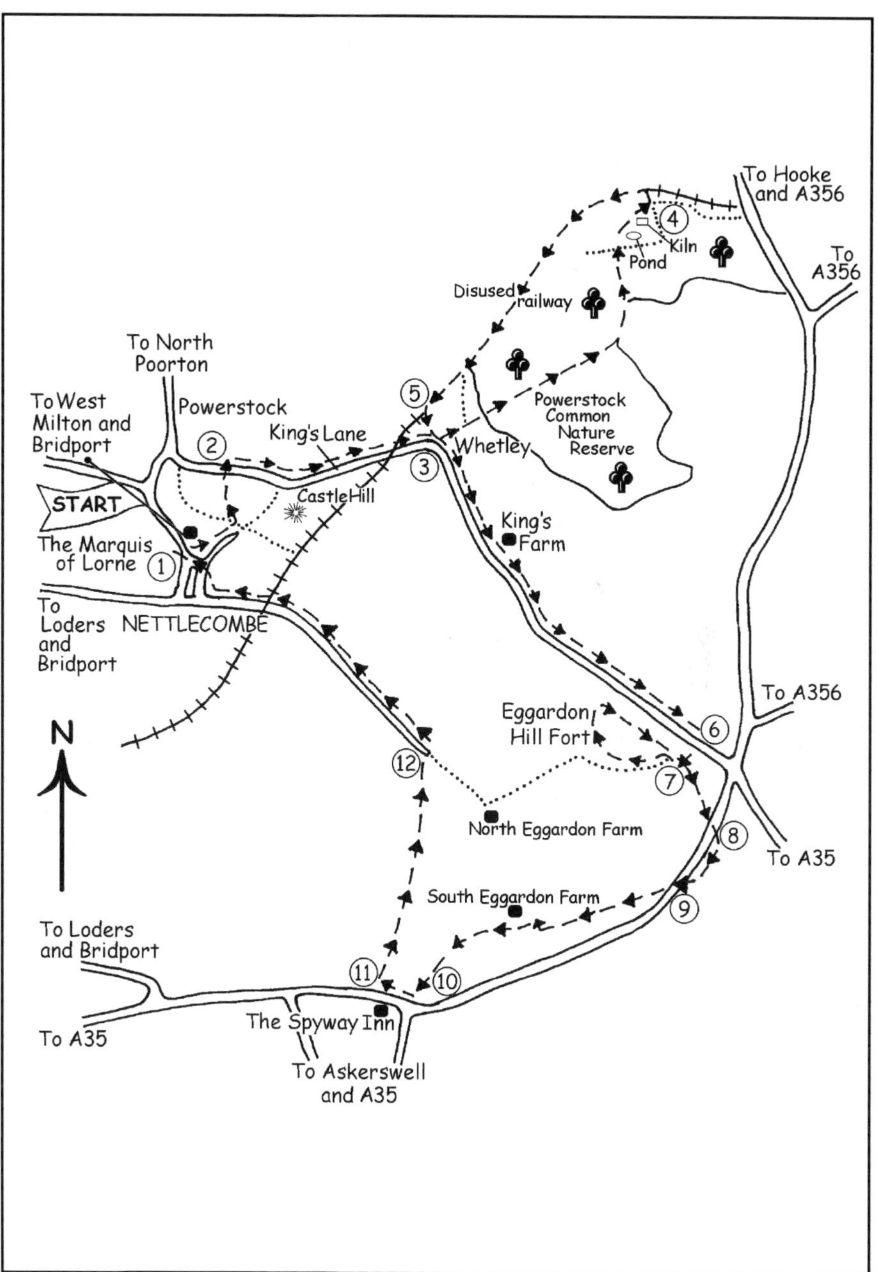
To Hooke and A356
To A356
Kiln
Pond
Disused railway
To North Poorton
To West Milton and Bridport
Powerstock
King's Lane
Whetley
Powerstock Common Nature Reserve
START
Castle Hill
The Marquis of Lorne
King's Farm
To Loders and Bridport
NETTLECOMBE
To A356
Eggardon Hill Fort
N
North Eggardon Farm
To A35
South Eggardon Farm
To Loders and Bridport
To A35
The Spyway Inn
To Askerswell and A35

This magnificent walk in west Dorset starts from Nettlecombe, an enchanting village of golden stone houses. From the village, tracks and lanes lead to the Dorset Wildlife Trust's Nature Reserve on Powerstock Common, once part of a royal forest. The reserve is a rich mosaic of ancient woodland, hazel coppice, open heathland, and grassy rides offering homes to a wide variety of wildlife. Roe and fallow deer rustle through the undergrowth and badgers dig their setts beneath the bracken.

Rising to the south of the reserve is one of Dorset's highest hills, Eggardon, its summit ringed by the ramparts of an Iron Age hill fort dating from around 300BC. We walk up to the fort and climb the ramparts to enjoy spectacular views south across the Marshwood Vale and Lyme Bay as far as Dartmoor and Start Point in Devon. Beyond the coastal hills there are glimpses of the sea. Downland paths and quiet lanes lead us back to Nettlecombe and the Marquis of Lorne inn.

The **Marquis of Lorne** inn was originally a farmhouse built in local golden stone in the 16th century. You cannot fail to enjoy your visit to this friendly, welcoming hostelry. The main bar, named after Eggardon, has blazing log fires in winter, mahogany panelling and walls decorated with a fascinating collection of old prints and photographs. There are two separate dining areas and a cosy snug, also named after local hills.

A wide range of tempting dishes were on offer when we called, including pan-fried breast of duck with fruits of the forest sauce, medallions of pork with onion and apple cream sauce and mussels in white wine topped with melted cheese. The real ales are Palmers IPA, 200 and Copper. There is a large, safe play area for children and beautiful gardens. This pub would make a perfect centre for a West Dorset holiday. Well-appointed accommodation is available and there is a self-catering cottage.

Opening times *are from 11.30 am to 2.30 pm and 6.30 pm to 11 pm. Food is served from 11.30 am to 2 pm and 6.30 pm to 9-9.30 pm in summer.*
On Sundays opening times are 12 noon to 3 pm and 7 pm to 10.30 pm with meals 12 noon to 2 pm and 7 pm to 9 pm.
Telephone: 01308 485236.

THE MARQUIS OF LORNE INN WAS ORIGINALLY A FARMHOUSE

The Walk

① Turn left from the front of the pub to walk down the lane. At the junction bear left past the no-through-road sign to walk through the village. The lane winds along the valley then drops downhill to a house and a signpost indicating several paths. Bear left following the sign '**Bridleway to Powerstock**' to cross a narrow footbridge over a stream and follow the narrow path ahead with the stream on your left. The path becomes a stony track leading uphill round the lower slopes of **Castle Hill**. The remains of the castle built by King John ring the summit but are concealed at this point by trees. The track meets **King's Lane**, also named after John.

② Turn right to follow this quiet lane sunk between banks and hung with hart's tongue ferns. It leads uphill and crosses a bridge over the track of the dismantled Maiden Newton to Bridport railway. Continue until you come to a sign '**Whetley Orchard**'. Alongside is a dilapidated fingerpost pointing left signed '**Bridleway to Stones Common**'.

③ Turn left through a gate and follow the path ahead past a house on the left and through two more gates, leaving a barn on your right. Walk straight up the middle of the meadow ahead and go through a small wooden gate leading into the woodland at the entrance to **Powerstock Common Nature Reserve**. Keep to the main path as it climbs uphill through woods of young oaks and runs over a more open area. Go straight over a crosstrack and through a gate to continue steeply uphill through more mixed woodlands. As you emerge from the woods follow the path round to the right to gain the highest point of the common and walk along a grassy bracken-fringed path. As the trees thin on your left you enjoy a fine view towards **Thorncombe Beacon** and **Golden Cap**. An avenue of weirdly twisted trees leads to an open expanse of wild flowers. Cross a wider track and follow the grassy path ahead through gates. Look for a small pool on your right dotted with lilies. Shortly after, also on your right, you come to the remains of a Suffolk-type brick kiln, dating from 1857. Continue over open grassland to a crosspath.

④ Turn left (indicated by a green arrow) and after about 30yds you come to the track of the former railway. Turn left to follow the track – now part of the reserve and a delightful walk.

The track runs through a deep cutting fragrant with wild flowers and plants attracting a wealth of butterflies in summer. These include Duke of Burgundy fritillaries, hairstreaks, marbled whites and skippers.

Continue for about 1½ miles. Pass a permissive path on your left and go under a bridge. About ½ mile further on you will see a large boulder on your right. Opposite is a stony track (unsigned).

⑤ Turn left down the track to rejoin **King's Lane**. Turn left to retrace your steps to **Whetley Orchard** then keep to the lane as it curves right and begins to climb steadily uphill past **King's Farm**. Follow the lane for about 1½ miles to the top of **Eggardon Hill** with wonderful views inland over the downs. At the top look for a bridleway sign by an iron gate.

⑥ Turn right through the gate, cross the grass ahead and go through another gate to a track.

⑦ Turn right for a few yards, go through a gate on your left and turn right again with a fence on your right to the highest ramparts of the Iron Age fort. Bear left to follow the ramparts around the southern and western rim of the fort, enjoying the splendid view, until you meet the fence again. Turn right with the fence on your left to cross the centre of the fort. Go through the gate and retrace your steps to point 7. Do not go through the gate on the left but keep straight on along the top of the ridge to meet a road.

This is a stretch of the road built by the Romans to run between the tribal capitals at Durnovaria (Dorchester) and Isca Dumnoniorum (Exeter).

⑧ Turn right for about 300yds to a gate and bridleway sign on the right.

⑨ Go through the gate and, bearing a little left, follow the embanked green path downhill and along the lower slopes of the hillside with a hedge on the right. Hedges appear on the left and a fence on the right as you see **South Eggardon Farm** in the valley on your right. Go through a gate and turn right downhill to a track. Turn left to leave the farm and all buildings on the right to continue through a gate, then, bearing a little left, follow a drive. This leads through another gate. Continue along the drive to meet the Roman road once more.

⑩ Turn right, passing the **Spyway Inn** on your left.

You may like to stop for refreshment at this old world inn. There is a comfortable bar and a separate restaurant with an amazing number of teacups hanging from the ceiling. Opening times are from 12 noon to 2.30 pm and from 6 pm to 11 pm. Meals are served from 12 noon to 2 pm and from 7 pm to 9 pm. Telephone: 01308 485250.

⑪ About 100yds past the inn you come to a stony track on the right (unsigned). Turn right up the track, keeping straight on when the track curves left to follow a grassy path between hedges. Continue beside a field with a hedge on the left then through fields to go through a gate. Keep straight on down a stony track to meet the drive to **North Eggardon Farm**.

⑫ Turn left following the sign for '**Powerstock ½**' (underestimated by at least a mile!). Follow the lane for about a mile, going under a railway bridge, and turn down a lane on the right to the junction in **Nettlecombe** village. Turn left up the lane to the **Marquis of Lorne** inn and your car.

Date walk completed:

Walk 4

CORSCOMBE AND BRACKETTS COPPICE NATURE RESERVE

MEDIEVAL CORSCOMBE COURT

Distance:
8 miles

Starting point:
*The Fox Inn's new car park or opposite the pub.
GR 526054*

Map: OS Explorer 117 Cerne Abbas and Bere Regis

How to get there: *Corscombe is about 4 miles north-east of Beaminster. Approach via the A356 Crewkerne to Dorchester road. Approaching from the south, turn off the A356 along the first lane on the right signed for the village. Coming from the north, pass the first lane signed for Corscombe and turn down the next (most easterly) lane for the village. Continue downhill, bearing left past the lane to the church and keeping straight on at the junction, following the sign for the Fox which appears shortly on your right.*

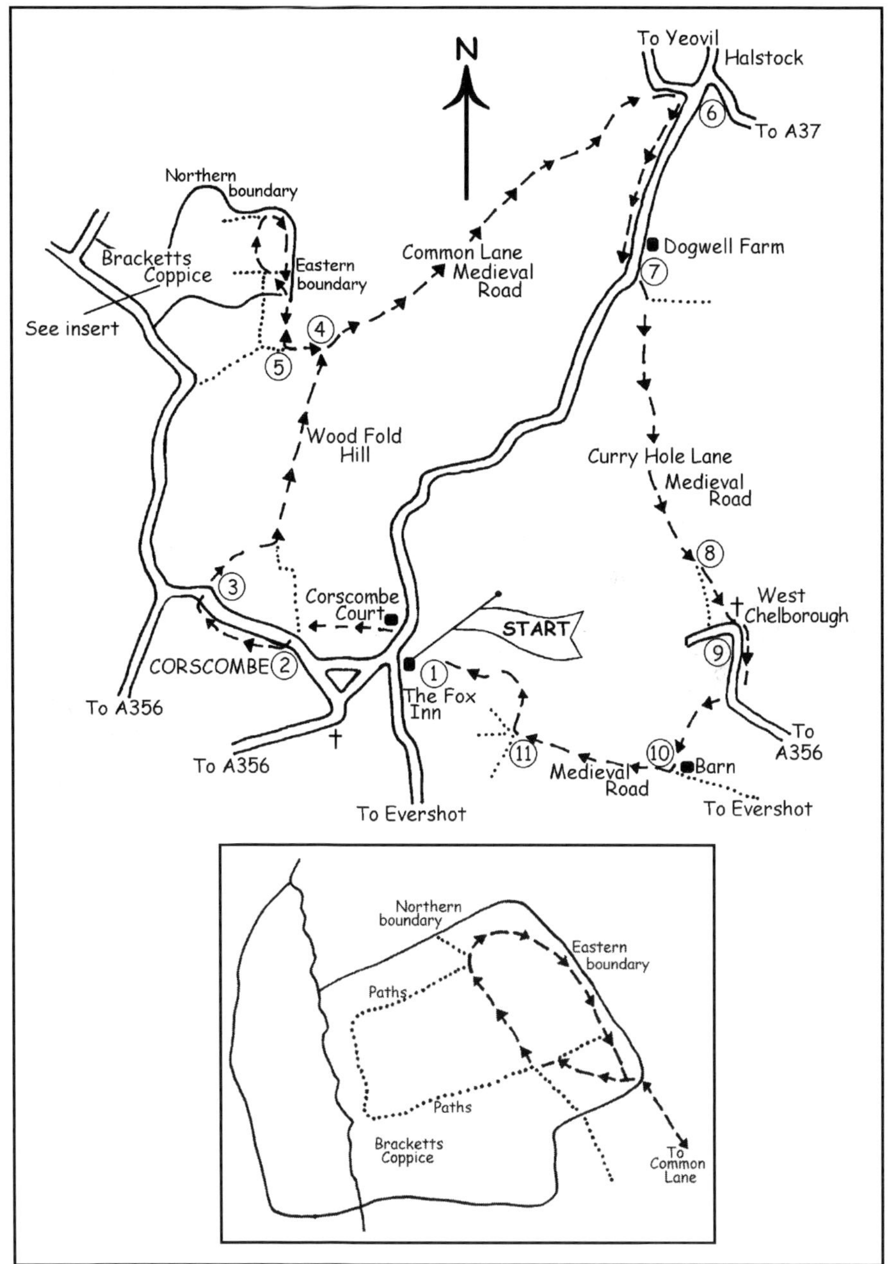
N
To Yeovil
Halstock
To A37
Northern boundary
Bracketts Coppice
Eastern boundary
See insert
Common Lane Medieval Road
Dogwell Farm
Wood Fold Hill
Curry Hole Lane Medieval Road
Corscombe Court
START
West Chelborough
CORSCOMBE
The Fox Inn
To A356
To A356
To A356
Barn
Medieval Road
To Evershot
To Evershot
Northern boundary
Eastern boundary
Paths
Paths
Bracketts Coppice
To Common Lane

This walk in north-west Dorset through the remote woods and hills surrounding the old world village of Corscombe is a step back in time. We follow cobbled medieval roads – once busy thoroughfares connecting scattered villages and hamlets, noisy with creaking wagons and the chatter of market folk. Now they are peaceful tracks exceptionally rich in wildlife. We begin the walk by heading north to Halstock, a small village with attractive mellow stone houses. On the way we make a short detour to explore Bracketts Coppice, a nature reserve where, again, time seems to have stood still. Part of the reserve is covered by ancient woodland, and is a Site of Special Scientific Interest. Another old road leads us south to West Chelborough, aptly described by Frederick Treves in his book *Highways and Byways in Dorset* as 'a delectable little place'. We return to Corscombe along a third medieval road, following the crest of a high ridge with glorious views.

Choose a summer day for the walk as this is the wettest part of Dorset and the paths can be quite muddy after prolonged rain.

Opposite medieval Corscombe Court stands the three hundred year old **Fox Inn**. Many travellers have found a kindly welcome and good food and ale in this picturesque thatched hostelry situated conveniently beside the old market road from Beaminster to Yeovil. It is also close to an ancient road running west from Evershot to Crewkerne, part of which we follow. Inside, the inn is just as you would expect, with low beams, flagged floors and huge fireplaces. There are two bars, a separate dining area and a conservatory.

Real ales are Exmoor Ale and Fox and Fuller's London Pride. Or you could sample Herefordshire cider, home-made elderflower cordial, damson vodka or sloe gin. There is an extensive and well-chosen wine list. When we called we found an impressive range of fish dishes: among them whole roast sea bass served with a tomato, olive and basil salad. Other dishes on offer included chicken breast stuffed with spinach and Boursin and rib-eye steak with a creamy horseradish sauce.

Opening times *are 12 noon to 3 pm and 7 pm to 11 pm. Meals are served from 12 noon to 2 pm and 7 pm to 9 pm (9.30 pm on Fridays and Saturdays). Accommodation is available.*
Telephone: 01935 891330.

① On leaving the front porch of the pub turn right and walk along the lane for about 50yds to a gateway on the left. (The footpath sign is on the other side of the road.) Turn left through a gate to pass **Corscombe Court Farm** and part of the moat on your right. Cross a stream and go through another gate to a field. There was no clear path at this point but cross the field, bearing a little left, keeping a hedge and fence on your left. In the far left-hand corner of the field you will find a stile. Cross this and keep ahead for about 30yds then turn left along a narrow path which dips over a gully. Cross a stile into a meadow – a colourful tapestry of wild flowers in summer. Bear a little left beside the meadow, keeping a hedge on your left, and go through a gate to a crosspath. Turn left for a few yards to the lane in **Corscombe** village.

② Turn right to walk through the village as far as an attractive house called **Pitt's Farm**.

③ Just after **Pitt's Farm**, before the road curves sharply left, turn right up a narrow lane which soon becomes cobbled. This is the first of our medieval roads, now known as **Common Lane**, linking **Corscombe** and **Halstock**. After about $^{1}/_{4}$ mile turn left at a crosstrack and follow **Common Lane** as it climbs **Wood Fold Hill**. The soft earth of the banks either side is honeycombed by badger setts. The track continues down the far side of the hill then climbs again shaded by oaks and beeches. As you gain height you come to a joining track on the left.

④ Turn left to follow this track through more open countryside for about 300yds to a footpath sign on the right.

⑤ Turn right through a gate and follow the wide grassy way ahead leading towards the trees of **Bracketts Coppice**. At the approach to the wood go through a gate, then turn immediately left through another gate to enter the coppice. (Ignore the 'Private' notice. The coppice now belongs to the Dorset Naturalists' Trust and visitors are welcome. Paths are indicated by yellow marks on short posts.) Follow the path through the bushes to emerge in more open woodland.

Among the wealth of wild flowers you will find early purple orchids and the unusual brownish bird's-nest orchid. Violets are the hosts for the caterpillars of several scarce fritillary butterflies. Swathes of honeysuckle provide nest building material for dormice and you may be lucky enough to see one – I did!

The path leads to a crosspath. Turn left for a few yards to a crosstrack. Turn right here along a wide way through old pasture grassland, with dense woods on your left. As you near the northern edge of the reserve leave the path, which continues to the boundary, and bear right, keeping the northern boundary about 100yds away through the trees on your left. After about 300yds, bear right again with the eastern boundary of the reserve visible through the trees on your left. As you walk bear a little right away from the trees to a yellow marked post. Keep ahead, due south, to walk through woods once more, ignoring all tracks to left and right. The path burrows through a coppice wood to our entrance path. Turn left to retrace your steps through the gates to return to **Common Lane** at point 4. Turn left to follow **Common Lane** to **Halstock**, bearing right to join the road through the village.

⑥ At the road junction turn right for **Corscombe**. Continue for about 3/4 mile to pass **Dogwell Farm**.

⑦ Turn left past the no-through-road sign to follow our second medieval road, now known as **Curry Hole Lane**, for about a mile, taking a higher path parallel with the track over a dip. Rejoin the track, cross a small wooden bridge and go through a gate to a meadow. The ground rises ahead, the track has vanished and there is no sign of a

THE THREE HUNDRED YEAR OLD FOX INN, CORSCOMBE

path. But walk up the slope and you will see **West Chelborough church** on the hillside ahead. Cross the meadow, aiming for the church, descend a slope and go through a wooden gate.

⑧ Tricky navigation here! Follow the mown path ahead for just a few yards then bear left into the long grass to turn immediately right and walk uphill with the mown path a few yards away on your right. After about 100yds, when you see the mown path beginning to curve right, keep straight on along a narrow path which suddenly becomes **Curry Hole Lane** again. Follow the track uphill through woodland to meet a lane by **West Chelborough church**.

⑨ Bear left to follow the lane for about $^1/_4$ mile. Leave the lane as it swings sharp left and turn right to cross a cattle grid and follow a track which rises through a gate. The track drops downhill to another gate in front of a yard with a barn on the left.

⑩ Turn right before the gate to follow our third medieval road along a grassy ridge running along the top of fields and through gates for about $^1/_2$ mile to a junction of five ways.

⑪ Turn right down a stony hedged track and go through a gate. Walk down the field ahead, hedge on right, to go through a gate into a wood. Follow the path, which turns left, to cross a gully to a gate opening into a field. Keeping the hedge close on your left walk up the field to a gate with a house a few yards away on the left. Go through the gate and turn immediately left uphill over a stile. After a few yards turn right to pass the house and grounds on your right. The path bears right to lead you over another stile. A path through trees brings you to open grassland. Continue along the narrow path over the grass towards the long thatched roof of the **Fox Inn** directly ahead. A final gate opens to a track to the right of the inn.

(According to the Dorset Wildlife Trust's brochure it is 'Bracketts' Coppice not 'Bracket's' Coppice as on the OS map. Also the notice on the gate into the reserve states it is owned by 'Dorset Naturalists' Trust', but they mean the same coppice!)

Date walk completed:

Walk 5

MAIDEN NEWTON AND THE VALLEY OF THE FROME

THE RIVER NEAR FROME VAUCHURCH

Distance:
$7\frac{1}{2}$ miles

Starting point:
Rock Pit Farm walkers' car park. GR 594978

Map: OS Explorer 117 Cerne Abbas and Bere Regis

How to get there: *Maiden Newton is about 8 miles north-west of Dorchester beside the A356. Drive into Maiden Newton on the A356 and turn up the minor road signed for Chilfrome. After about $\frac{1}{4}$ mile the car park is on your left.*

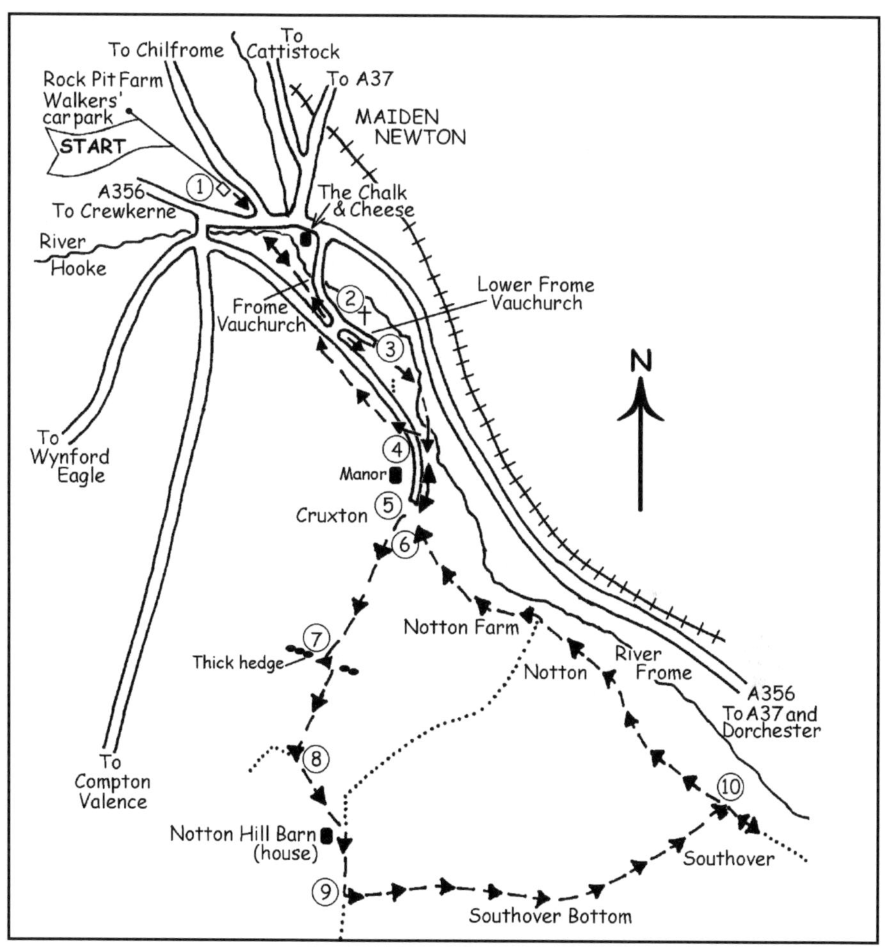

The A356 road carries heavy traffic through the centre of Maiden Newton and at first glance the village appears to be too busy to be interesting. But wander down some of the quiet side streets and you will discover the appeal of this old fashioned riverside village. I suggest a stroll down Church Street past the stump of the 15th-century market cross. On your right is the Old School dating from1840. William Barnes' poem *The Fancy Fair at Maiden Newton* was sold at the fair to raise funds to build the school. The clock with its swinging pendulum was added in 1887 to celebrate Queen Victoria's Diamond Jubilee.

North of Dorchester the river Frome has carved a beautiful valley through the chalk downland. This walk explores one of the loveliest areas of the valley around Maiden Newton, a large village cradled in the downs at the confluence of the Frome and the little river Hooke. From the village, the route runs through the meadows beside the river. This clear chalk stream flows sparkling between banks colourful with wild flowers. Occasionally you may glimpse the turquoise flash of a kingfisher or the conspicuous white bib of a dipper.

A peaceful lane leads through hamlets of attractive flint and stone banded houses before we climb the downs and follow a ridge with splendid views. A long descent down a wide grassy coombe brings us back to the river, which we follow to return to Maiden Newton.

After passing some attractive Georgian houses and rows of old world cottages you come to the church, which dates mainly from the 12th century. In the north wall a Norman door still hangs on its original hinges.

Opposite Church Street, beside the main road, stands the Victorian village pub, the **Chalk & Cheese**. The name seems highly appropriate as a chalk stream runs close by and Dorset is famous for its Blue Vinney cheese! This is a real village pub with a warm and friendly atmosphere and a special welcome for walkers. As well as a cosy bar there are comfortable eating areas with sturdy wooden tables and deep cushioned window seats. Real ales are Bass and Flowers and up to three guest ales. Home-cooked meals on offer when we called included pan-fried chicken supreme, spaghetti bolognaise, and a selection of savoury pies and puddings. We were tempted by chicken, ham and mushroom pudding but finally settled for their splendid all-day breakfast. Desserts included fresh lemon treacle sponge and apple and blackberry popovers. Teas and coffees come with a home-made cake. A real feature of this pub is the delightful walled garden with a view over the river valley. There is also a separate sun terrace.

The pub is open *Monday to Thursday 11 am to 3 pm and 6 pm to 11 pm. Friday and Saturday it is open all day from 11 am to 11 pm, Sunday from 12 noon to 10.30 pm. Meals are served from 12 noon to 2.30 pm and from 6 pm to 8.30 pm. No food is served on Tuesdays.*
Telephone: 01300 320600.

THE VICTORIAN VILLAGE PUB IN MAIDEN NEWTON

The Walk

① Turn left from the car park entrance to walk down the road towards the A356. Cross the A356 and follow the footpath sign straight ahead over a footbridge. Immediately you are in countryside with cows grazing peacefully on the river bank. Follow the path ahead over a meadow and go through two gates. The path now follows the river bank with grassy hillsides rising on your right. The hills on your left beyond the river are terraced with strip lynchets, long narrow fields ploughed by land-hungry farmers in the 13th century. Go through a gate on your left to a lane and turn right. Continue along the lane through the small hamlet of **Frome Vauchurch**.

② When the lane bends right (signed for **Cruxton**) keep straight on along the lane marked with a no-through-road sign for **Lower Frome Vauchurch**. The name 'Frome Vauchurch' means 'Estate on the River Frome with a coloured church' and you pass the little church with its enormous bell on your left. Dedicated to St Francis, the atmosphere inside the church is unbelievably restful. An ancient carved wooden reredos hangs on one of the walls.

③ The lane ceases as you pass the last house in **Lower Frome Vauchurch**. Keep straight on over a meadow. The path curves right and left as it crosses the meadow then goes through a wide gap in a thick hedge. At this point the path divides. Keep ahead (left hand path) to go over a stile and cross the river over a wooden footbridge. A narrow path leads through trees and over an old sluice gate. Follow the narrow path ahead to a stile which brings you to a field. Turn right – the river is now on your right – along the edge of the field to a gate on your right. Go through the gate and cross a bridge over a glorious stretch of the river to rejoin the lane.

④ Turn left to follow the lane to **Cruxton**. You pass **Cruxton Manor**, a fine Tudor house with mullioned windows, on your right. At the end of the lane go through a gate by a sign '**Notton Unsuitable for Motors**'.

⑤ Climb the white track ahead and go through the next gate. The track bears left for a few yards to a signpost.

⑥ Turn right, following the sign for **Compton Valence**, to climb the hillside. As you gain height you are rewarded by beautiful views over the **Frome valley**. The track levels to run beside meadows. After you have climbed for about $^1/_2$ mile you come to a thick hedge either side of the track.

⑦ Navigate carefully here as the route differs slightly from the OS map. Do not continue through the hedge but turn left, with the hedge on your right, for a few yards then follow the track as it curves right through another gap. Keep ahead now with a hedge on your right for about $^1/_4$ mile to a stile and signpost.

⑧ Turn left, following the sign for **Notton Hill Barn**, with a hedge on your right along the edge of a field. Cross a stile and walk over the large field ahead along a narrow path towards a wood. When you reach the trees, **Notton Hill Barn** – a large house – is on your right. Cross a track, following the sign for **Compton Valence**, and after a few yards turn right to follow a grassy path with a hedge on your left. On your right a parallel track runs to some outbuildings. Follow the grassy path as it drops downhill to a gate.

⑨ Go through the gate and turn left to follow a winding path down the valley. This glorious coombe, known by the unassuming name of **Southover Bottom**, is a beautiful, remote, gently sloping valley and is one of my favourite places in Dorset. The path leads through gates, continuing for over a mile to bring you to a white crosstrack. Beyond the track the **Frome** is hidden by dense bushes and trees.

⑩ Our way is left here through a gate but first I suggest you make a short detour to see **Southover** village. So turn right for a few yards. Dark roofs of heavy thatch overhang houses built of dove-grey flint and stone and colourful gardens overflow into the road. Retrace your steps and go through the gate signed for **Notton**. Follow the path, with the river through the trees on your right, through more gates for almost a mile. Just past a barn on your left keep to the same track as it curves right downhill. At the foot of the descent the track bears left to resume its original heading, north-west. Over a cattle grid the track becomes asphalt with grass down the middle and brings you to **Notton**. Keep to the track as it curves left for **Cruxton**, ignoring the track on the right, to pass **Notton Farm** on your left. The track continues through gates downhill between steep hillsides then rises to meet our outbound route at point 6. Retrace your steps, turning right after a few yards through the gate, downhill into **Cruxton** then following the lane past the manor to the bridge and footpath sign at point 4. Here you have a choice of routes. If you wish you could turn right over the bridge and retrace your steps over the fields to return to **Maiden Newton** or you could continue along the lane. If you prefer to follow the lane keep ahead to a road junction and turn right for **Maiden Newton**. At the T-junction in **Frome Vauchurch** turn left. Retrace your outbound route, turning left through the gate to take the field footpath just before you come to the large bridge on your right.

To visit the Chalk & Cheese turn right when you meet the A356 and cross the bridge. The pub is a few yards further on your right.

Date walk completed:

Walk 6

PORTESHAM, THE HARDY MONUMENT AND LITTLEBREDY

BRIDEHEAD HOUSE, LITTLEBREDY

Distance:
8 miles

Starting point:
The King's Arms car park. GR 603857

Map: OS Outdoor Leisure 15 Purbeck and South Dorset

How to get there: *Portesham lies beside the B3157 about 7 miles west of Weymouth. The King's Arms is at the south end of the village on the main road.*

The countryside of Dorset is so beautiful and varied that you can walk almost anywhere and be rewarded with marvellous views. But one of the finest must be the one you enjoy on this walk from the top of Black Down Hill. Rising to 780ft this former beacon hill is the highest point on the Dorset Ridgeway. Inland, rolling chalk downland reaches to the fringes of Cranborne Chase. To the east are the Purbeck hills and to the west the whole Dorset coast is visible as far as Start Point in Devon. Crowning the hill is a tall chimney-shaped monument commemorating Sir Thomas Masterman Hardy, captain of Nelson's flagship *Victory* at the battle of Trafalgar.

Woodland paths lead to Littlebredy, a tranquil cluster of thatched cottages hidden in a magical valley, and the beautiful gardens surrounding Bridehead, a great house built in classical style at the source of the river Bride. High downland paths bring us back to Portesham, a grey stone village tucked in a coombe in the coastal downs, our starting point for this walk.

Portesham is proud of its famous former resident, Admiral Hardy, and you will find many reminders of him inside the village pub, the **King's Arms**. From the windows you can see Hardy's boyhood home, Portesham House. Part of the spacious bar area is designed as a replica of his cabin on board *Victory*. The captain was a tall man and liked to imagine he could see the sky so the ceiling included a false skylight painted with stars.

There is a large separate restaurant and a family room. Two real ales are always on offer, one of which is Flowers Original. Appetising home-cooked dishes when we called included chicken, bacon and tarragon pie, and a Mexican platter – chilli served with spicy chicken wings and a salsa and sour cream dip. The fish menu included pearl snapper and fresh crab salad. To follow you will be tempted by a choice of delicious trifles, cheesecakes and fruit pies. There is a pleasant streamside garden.

Opening times *are from 11 am to 11 pm in summer and meals are served from 12 noon to 9 pm. Out of summer the hours are: Monday to Saturday 11 am to 2.30 pm and 6.30 pm to 11 pm, Sunday 12 noon to 3 pm and 7 pm to 10.30 pm, and food is served from 12 noon to 2 pm and from 6.30 pm to 9 pm; and all day on Sunday.*
Telephone: 01305 871342.

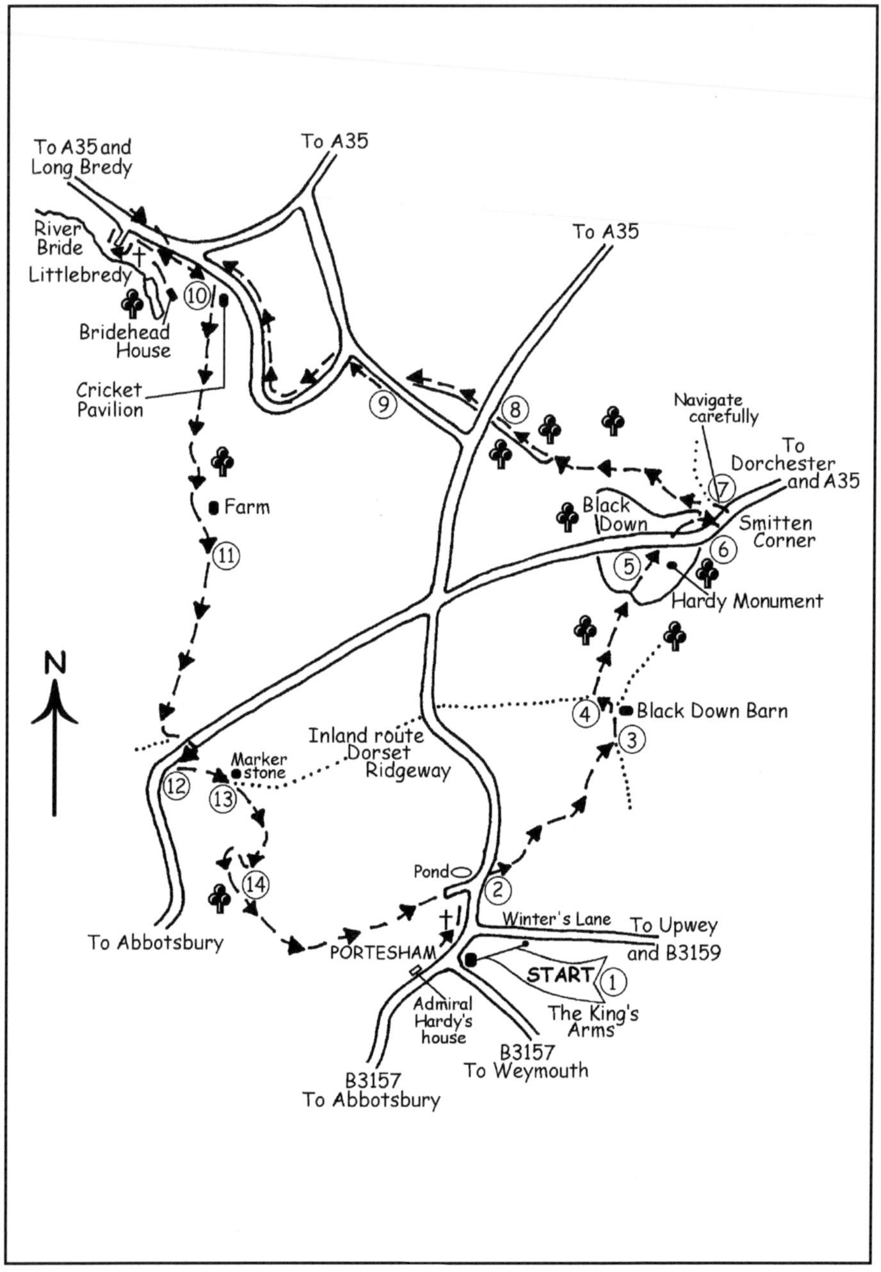
To A35 and Long Bredy
To A35
To A35
River Bride
Littlebredy
Bridehead House
Cricket Pavilion
Farm
Navigate carefully
To Dorchester and A35
Black Down
Smitten Corner
Hardy Monument
Black Down Barn
Inland route Dorset Ridgeway
Marker stone
N
Pond
Winter's Lane
To Upwey and B3159
START
The King's Arms
PORTESHAM
Admiral Hardy's house
To Abbotsbury
B3157 To Weymouth
B3157 To Abbotsbury
1
2
3
4
5
6
7
8
9
10
11
12
13
14

① Turn right from the **King's Arms** car park to the corner where the B3157 turns left for **Abbotsbury**. Across the road stands **Portesham House**, solidly built of grey stone. Most of the exterior dates from the 18th and 19th centuries but the core of the building is a 16th-century farmhouse.

Hardy went to sea as 'captain's servant' at the age of twelve. In 1793 he was Lieutenant aboard the frigate* Meleager*. He was given command of* Victory *in 1803. All his life he retained his love for Portesham and for all things made in Dorset. He never went to sea until his ship was well supplied with Dorset cheese and beer!

Turn right to leave the B3157 and walk up **Front Street**, passing the school and church on your left. The church, dedicated to St Peter, dates from the 12th century and has many fascinating features including a massive 16th-century folding door with its original lock. Continue past the road to **Upwey** on the right and follow the road as it curves right past the village store to a bridleway on the right signed '**Hardy Monument**'.

② Turn right up the tree-shaded track and go through a gate leading to open downland. Ignore the footpath on the right and keep straight ahead up the down with a hedge on your left. At the top of the rise the path bears right with a wall on your left. Already there are wide views of hillsides, scored with strip lynchets made by land-hungry medieval farmers and dotted with round burial mounds dating from the Bronze Age, some four thousand years ago. The track curves left between stone walls then bears right with a wall on the right. Go through a gate and directly ahead you will see the **Hardy Monument**. Keep ahead with the wall still on your right as the track runs downhill to another gate and a crosstrack.

③ Through the gate turn left to descend into the valley, passing the ruins of **Black Down Barn** on your right. Just past the barn ignore the bridleway on the right for **Smitten Corner** and bear left, with trees on your right, to a signpost '**Inland route Hardy Monument**'.

④ Turn right to walk uphill through the woods following the '**Hardy Monument**' signs. Leave the woods to bear a little right up the hillside to the monument and enjoy the superb view!

The monument is open from April to September, Saturdays and

Sundays from 1 pm to 5 pm. A winding staircase leads to the top.

⑤ Follow the track from the monument to a road, turn right for a few yards, then turn left along a narrow footpath signed 'Inland route avoiding road'. This winds along the hillside then runs down to a stile. Cross the stile and walk downhill through a wood to cross another stile. Follow the path ahead to meet the road again.

⑥ Turn left for about 30yds to **Smitten Corner** then turn left to enter **Black Down Forest**, following the bridleway sign for **Littlebredy**. Navigate carefully now! Continue along the broad, inviting track for only about 100yds.

⑦ Look for a less obvious joining track up a slope on your left. There is no sign but this really is the bridleway to **Littlebredy**. Leave the broad track (which shortly curves right downhill) and turn left up the slope to keep your height and follow a delightful grassy way through mixed woodland. Leave the trees and follow the path, with woods still on your left, and open downland on your right, to a road.

⑧ Cross the road and follow the bridleway ahead, with woods still on your left, to meet a lane. (The sign for our bridleway from the lane is rather oddly placed a few yards over the heath among the brambles on your right.)

⑨ Turn right beside the lane for about 300yds then turn left down the very narrow lane (cycle route sign) leading down into the **Littlebredy valley**, curving right past **Littlebredy Farm**. Continue along the lane for about $^{1}/_{2}$ mile. The lane curves left to give views of Bridehead House. Just past the cricket pavilion on your left is the bridleway we shall follow later in the walk. But first, keep ahead along the lane and turn left down a narrow path leading through the churchyard to the church. Pass the side of the church on your right then bear left for a few yards to a path on the right leading into the grounds of **Bridehead House**.

You can walk in the grounds free of charge but you are invited to put a contribution in the church box. The grounds are really beautiful with grassy banks dotted with fine trees sloping down to a lake and miniature waterfall.

Retrace your steps towards the church and, passing the south porch on your right, follow the path past a row of thatched cottages to a lane. Turn right uphill then right again to return to the bridleway mentioned above just before the cricket pavilion.

⑩ Turn right through a gate, passing the pavilion on your left. The track leads uphill through another gate. When the track curves right, keep straight ahead up a grassy path. The path climbs the hillside then bears a little left to run beside trees and a fence on the left past a farm. Bear left to go through two gates and keep straight ahead, with a fence on the left, to go through another gate.

⑪ Bearing slightly right follow the track ahead for over $^{1}/_{2}$ mile to a crosstrack. Turn left and after a few yards turn left again to a narrow road.

⑫ Turn right for about 300yds to a sign on the left marked '**Hardy Monument**'. Turn left through a small gate and follow the path as it curves round the crest of a coombe to a marker stone.

⑬ Bear right for **Portesham** along a very narrow path, aiming for the crest of the ridge ahead and keeping a fence on your left. Follow the line of the fence as it descends to a corner. Turn right, still following the line of the fence and keeping it on your left along the crest of the ridge. After about 80yds follow the fence round to the left, a little downhill, to a signpost. Turn right for **Portesham**, walking down into the valley. The path then curves left to bring you to a gate in front of a wood.

⑭ Go through the gate and follow the path along the valley with the wood on your right. When the wood ends go through a gate and keep ahead, with a fence on your right, to go through two gates. At the top of the field turn right through a small gate along the narrow hedged path, signed for **Portesham**. The path runs right to a lane in **Portesham**. Turn left past the village pond then right down **Front Street** to return to the **King's Arms**.

Date walk completed:

Walk 7

LANGTON HERRING, THE CHESIL BEACH AND THE FLEET LAGOON

THE BEACH NEAR LANGTON HIVE POINT

Distance:
$7\frac{1}{2}$ miles

Starting point:
The Elm Tree Inn car park. The inn has set aside a large parking area – the Paddock – for patrons who wish to walk. Turn right towards the inn then immediately right again into the Paddock.
GR 614825

Map: OS Outdoor Leisure 15 Purbeck and South Dorset

How to get there: *Langton Herring is a mile west of the B3157 about 3 miles west of Weymouth. Turn off the B3157, following the sign for the village, then turn left, following the sign for the Elm Tree Inn, which is on your right.*

The Chesil Beach is a unique feature of the Dorset coast. This sturdy bank of pebbles links Portland with West Bay, defying the force of the Atlantic waves and the prevailing south-westerly winds for over 17 miles. Trapped behind it lies the Fleet, 8 miles long, the largest tidal lagoon in Britain. Immensely rich in wildlife, most of this fascinating area is now a nature reserve. From Langton Herring we follow the Coast Path beside the Fleet shore for 4 miles then turn inland to cross the downs back to the village. As in most coastal villages, the inhabitants of Langton Herring took an active part in the trade of smuggled goods from the Continent during the 18th and early 19th centuries. Many battles between smugglers and the Revenue men took place on the Chesil Beach and the deadly undertow wrecked many ships. These are the themes of J. Meade Falkner's exciting novel *Moonfleet*. The walk passes the manor of the Mohun family who have lent their name to the novel, and visits East Fleet, the home of its hero John Trenchard.

This is a walk you can enjoy at all times of the year. Remember to take your binoculars as the Fleet is one of the best places in southern England for observing birds.

Langton Herring is a small village sheltered from the sea by a ridge of downland. Many of the older houses are built of golden stone and thatched. One of the oldest must be the attractive village pub, the **Elm Tree**. It dates from 1265 and part of the original building is still intact. Low ceilings crossed by huge beams and walls decorated with shining brass and copper contribute to the pub's old world atmosphere and it is easy to imagine a group of local men planning their next smuggling venture in the dark recesses of its large inglenook fireplace. A bricked-up hole in the cellar is possibly an escape tunnel or a hiding place for contraband.

Real ales are 6X, Bass and Flowers and the cider is Blackthorn. When we called the interesting and varied menu included fillet steak with a Stilton sauce, Barbury duck breast with a red cherry compote, fillet of sea bass and pan-fried scallops with lemon.

Opening times *on Monday to Saturday are 11.30 am to 3 pm and 6.30 pm to 11.30 pm. Sunday hours are 12 noon to 3 pm and 7 pm to 10.30 pm. Food is served 12 noon to 2 pm and 7 pm to 9 pm.*
Telephone: 01305 871257.

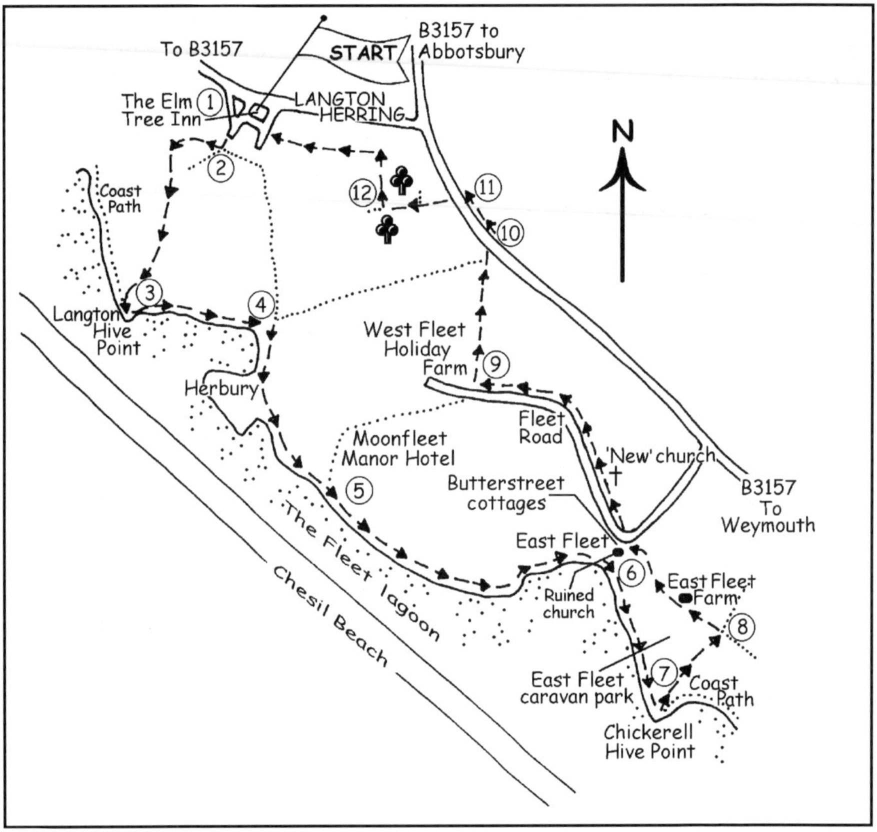

The Walk

① Leave the front of the pub and turn right. Almost immediately turn right again. The lane curves right past the little church of St Peter which, like the inn, dates from the 13th century. A horse chestnut tree has been planted in the churchyard in memory of Sir Winston Churchill. The lane curves left, passing a turning on the right, to bring you to a T-junction. Turn left and walk uphill.

② Ignore the footpath signs ahead and keep to the track as it swings right to follow a high ridge with splendid views over the valleys and woodlands of the coastal downs. The track curves left towards the sea to give you your first view of **the**

Fleet, protected by the **Chesil Beach**. Follow the track as it descends past a small wood on the left then bears right past a line of coastguard's cottages towards the shore. On the left is the footpath sign for the **Dorset Coast Path**. Continue past the sign down the slipway to **Langton Hive Point**. 'Hive' means a landing place and small boats used for fishing are drawn up on the beach.

③ Retrace your steps to the **Coast Path** signpost and turn right through a gate following the sign '**Moonfleet and Ferrybridge**'. The path runs along the foot of fields with wide views over **the Fleet** on your right.

Among the waterfowl enjoying this quiet lagoon you will see mute swans, first settled here by the monks at Abbotsbury, and Brent geese, recognisable by their dark heads and necks and white collars. Groups of goldeneye can be distinguished by their characteristic white spot beneath the eye and wigeon by their reddish-brown plumage. Other common birds include oystercatchers, dunlin and redshank. Tall grey herons stand fishing at the water's edge. Each spring some of our rarest birds, little terns, nest on the Chesil Beach, disguising their eggs among the pebbles. You may see one dive to seize a tiny fish in its

THE ELM TREE INN, LANGTON HERRING

orange beak, wings gracefully arched above its back.

④ Cross a wooden footbridge and walk up to a signpost. Turn right, following the sign for **Ferrybridge**, keeping a wall on your left over the neck of the Herbury peninsula. Over a stile the path bears left. Follow the edge of the field with the hedge on your right. The bank slopes steeply down to the shore on your right. Cross the next stile, go over a plank bridge and follow the path as it curves right through the hedge then left along the clifftop. Keep to the **Coast Path** as it runs past the track to **Moonfleet Manor Hotel** – originally Fleet House – on your left.

You may like to pause here for refreshment. Walkers are welcome.

⑤ Keep ahead over a field. Cross a stile, a small bridge and a wooden walkway and climb some steps. Turn right for **East Fleet** along the edge of a field which slopes gently upwards on your left. The waters of **the Fleet** are again close on your right. Go through a gate and keep ahead along the side of a wide mown gallop. We walked this way in June and the fields were brilliant with scarlet poppies and white moon daisies. Follow the gallop as it curves a few yards left then right, then leave it to keep straight on through the bushes and down some steps. Cross a plank bridge, go over a stile and continue ahead over another stile to **East Fleet**.

Only the chancel of the church and a single row of cottages, Butterstreet, survived the great storm of November 1824. Chesil Beach was inundated and waves swept across the lagoon and up the village street 'as fast as a horse could gallop'. To see the remains of the church featured in Falkner's novel leave the Coast Path and turn left. Cross the bridge on your right by the churchyard wall and walk round to a gate into the churchyard on your left. The vault where the smugglers concealed their casks among the Mohun tombs lies under the chancel floor. On each side of the altar are two fine brasses to members of the Mohun family and a plaque in memory of Falkner.

⑥ Continue heading east along the **Coast Path**, over stiles and bridges, past the southern boundary of **East Fleet caravan site** to a gravel track leading down to the landing stage at **Chickerell Hive Point**.

⑦ Turn left, signed for **Chickerell**, and walk uphill to cross a stile to a lane.

⑧ Turn left down the lane to the caravan site at **East Fleet Farm**.

Pass the pub and shop on your right and keep straight ahead up the lane. The lane curves left downhill to pass **Butterstreet** cottages. Keep to the lane as it swings right to **Fleet Road**. Turn left and walk up the road past the 'new' church built in 1829. The tower houses the bell from the old church destroyed in the storm.

⑨ At the top of the hill turn right along the concrete track past the entrance to **West Fleet Holiday Farm**. Do not enter the farm but keep to the concrete track as it curves right. After a few yards, when the concrete track swings left, keep straight ahead due north along a pleasant grass-bordered way which dips then climbs to meet the B3157.

⑩ Turn left along the grass and follow the road for about 300yds until the road dips and you come to a small gravel layby beside a belt of trees on your left.

⑪ Look carefully on your left for a bridleway sign and small wooden gate half-hidden in the trees. Turn left through the gate and follow a narrow path through the trees with a deep gully hung with ferns on your left. Pass a track leading to a field on your right and continue for about 1/4 mile until you can see the end of the belt of woodland about 50yds ahead.

⑫ At this point there is a track leading uphill on your right (no sign). Turn right to follow this through woods and round a left hand bend. The track leaves the woods to run across fields past a turning on the right towards **Langton Herring**. Continue over a wide farmyard and through a gate. Follow the stony track ahead to the road in the centre of the village and turn right to return to the **Elm Tree Inn**.

Date walk completed:

Walk 8

SHERBORNE AND SANDFORD ORCAS

SANDFORD ORCAS MANOR, PASSED ON THE WALK

Distance:
10 miles

Starting point:
Culverhayes car park.
GR 641164

Map: OS Explorer 129 Yeovil and Sherborne

How to get there: *Sherborne can be reached via the A30 or the A352. From the A352 go along the B3145. Turn down Gas House Hill, cross the railway and take the next road on the right, Ludbourne Road, following the car park sign. Turn left into the car park.*

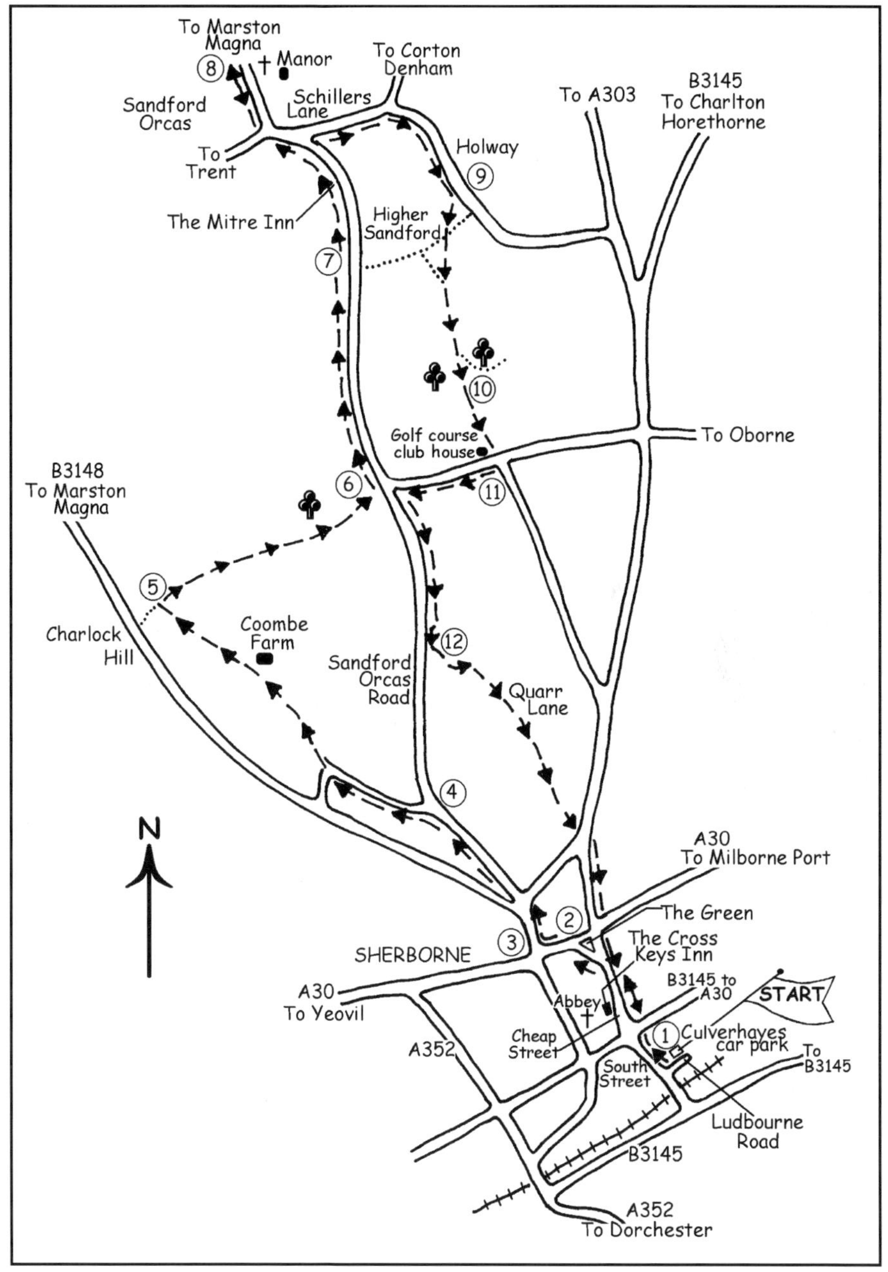
To Marston Magna
Manor
To Corton Denham
8
Sandford Orcas
Schillers Lane
To A303
B3145 To Charlton Horethorne
To Trent
Holway
9
The Mitre Inn
Higher Sandford
7
10
Golf course club house
To Oborne
B3148 To Marston Magna
6
11
5
Charlock Hill
Coombe Farm
12
Sandford Orcas Road
Quarr Lane
4
N
A30 To Milborne Port
The Green
2
3
The Cross Keys Inn
SHERBORNE
B3145 to A30
START
A30 To Yeovil
Abbey
1
Culverhayes car park
A352
Cheap Street
To B3145
South Street
Ludbourne Road
B3145
A352 To Dorchester

This walk starts in Sherborne, an exquisite town in the north of the county not far from the border with Somerset. Built of honey-coloured Ham Hill stone, the town is beautifully sited at the foot of wooded hills beside the river Yeo. We begin with a ramble through some of the historic streets close to Sherborne's magnificent Abbey Church, founded by St Aldhelm in AD 705. Then, a complete contrast! The bustling streets are quickly left behind as we follow quiet lanes and paths to the head of a remote valley to enjoy a wonderful view over Somerset with Cadbury Castle a dark shape on the horizon. Half-hidden in a dell lies our destination, Sandford Orcas, one of Dorset's timeless villages. Here a Tudor manor house with an equally old church at its gates overlooks a scattering of houses and cottages, many as old as the manor, with mullioned windows and roofs of stone or thatch.

We leave Sandford Orcas along another lovely valley and climb for more splendid views before returning to Sherborne along an old cobbled lane.

Sherborne's Abbey Church became part of a Benedictine monastery at the end of the 10th century. At the Dissolution of the Monasteries in 1539, the church, newly-completed in the late Gothic style we admire today, was saved from destruction by the vicar and townspeople, who bought it for £320! Not far from the Abbey Close in The Parade stands the monks' washroom, known as the Conduit, a many sided building with open Gothic arches. This originally stood in the cloister court of the monastery and was moved to its present position in the heart of the town at the Dissolution. Overlooking the Conduit and the market square you will find the excellent pub I have chosen for this walk, the **Cross Keys**. This is a welcoming, traditional Dorset pub dating, like the Abbey, from the 15th century. There is plenty of room for families and quiet corners if you wish. Real ales are Hardy Country, Royal Oak and Bass and a guest beer. Cider is Blackthorn and there is an extensive wine list. If you fancy a lighter meal the pub offers delicious paninis, toasted ciabatta bread with a variety of fillings including brie and bacon. Home-made 'specials' change daily and among the dishes on offer when we called were large gammon steaks, a tasty 'sausage and mash' and tuna and mixed pepper lasagne. On Sundays there is a choice of two roasts. In fine weather you can sit at tables outside the pub in the Square and watch the world go by. The scene is particularly lively on Saturday, when the Square is crammed with a colourful array of market stalls. It is wise to book your meal in advance! The Cross Keys offers accommodation.

Opening times *are from 11 am to 11 pm every day except Sunday, when the hours are from 12 noon to 10.30 pm. In summer meals are served from 12 noon to 8 pm and in winter from 12 noon to 2 pm and from 6 pm to 8 pm. Telephone: 01935 812492.*

The Walk

① Turn right from the car park entrance then right again to walk up **South Street**. On your left you will see the **Church House**, a rare survival, built 1532-4 with shops below and one long room above. Here festivities known as 'Church Ales' were once held to provide funds for the upkeep of the church. Pass the entrance to the **Abbey Close**, the **Conduit** and the **Cross Keys** pub and keep ahead up **Cheap Street**. Follow the road as it curves left, passing the **White Hart** pub at **The Green**, to the A30.

② Turn left down the raised walkway beside the A30. At the foot of the hill cross the road in front of the **Crown Inn** and continue with the A30 on your left.

③ Turn right beside the B3148 **Marston Magna** road to pass **Sherborne International Study Centre** on your right. Just past the study centre, at the fork, take the lane on the right signed '**Coombe**'.

The building on your right with a 14th-century window was formerly a chapel dedicated to St Emerentiana, a Roman martyr of unknown date. According to legend a mob found her praying beside the tomb of her foster sister, St Agnes, and stoned her to death.

All signs of the town are quickly left behind as you follow the lane winding gradually uphill between grassy hillsides.

④ After about $^1/_2$ mile, as the road swings right by the sign for **Sandford Orcas** (this does not indicate the village itself, which is 3 miles further on), turn left just past a thatched house, up a narrow, deeply-hedged lane still leading you gradually up the valley. When another lane joins on the left keep straight on along a track. Go through a gate and now, as you near the head of the valley, a field path leads you across a grassy dip in the hills and through another gate. The path runs straight ahead with a hedge close on the right and a bank shaded by tall lime trees on the left. Continue through more gates past **Coombe Farm** and some pretty cottages to the top of **Charlock Hill**.

⑤ Turn right along a delightful track running high along the crest of a ridge. As you turn the corner there are fine views northwards over Somerset. Later the track is bordered by massive trees and at one point sinks deep between their knotted roots, forming a miniature gorge. As the track leaves the gorge and gains height wide views over the Dorset downs unfold to the south. After about a mile the track descends through a gate into a beautiful wooded valley and curves left to meet the **Sandford Orcas** road.

⑥ Turn left and follow the road to **Sandford Orcas**. (Do not be misled by the distance on the signpost – you can add a mile.) The lane drops downhill and ahead you will see the village cupped in the hills.

⑦ Continue past the houses in **Higher Sandford** and follow the road as it curves right and left through **Sandford Orcas** past the **Mitre Inn**.

THE 15TH-CENTURY CROSS KEYS PUB IN SHERBORNE

The Mitre is an attractive country pub. It is open Monday to Saturday from 11.30 am to 2.30 pm and from 7 pm to 11 pm. Meals are served from 12 noon to 2 pm and from 7 pm to 9.30 pm. No food is served on Monday evenings. Opening hours on Sunday are from 12 noon to 3 pm and from 7 pm to 10.30 pm. Meals are served from 12 noon to 2 pm and from 7 pm to 9 pm.

After passing **Schillers Lane** on your right and the road to **Trent** on your left you come to the church overlooking the drive leading to the gatehouse at the entrance to **Sandford Orcas Manor**.

This charming Tudor house has survived the centuries practically unaltered, retaining almost all its original windows, fireplaces and spiral staircases. It is the home of the Medlycott family, who share their property with no fewer than 35 ghosts! The Manor is open Easter Monday 10 am to 5 pm and in May, July, August and September it is open Sundays and Mondays 2 pm-5 pm. Telephone: 01963 220206.

⑧ Retrace your steps to the corner of **Schillers Lane** and turn left, signed for **Holway**. After about 1/4 mile turn right, still following the sign for **Holway**. Shortly the lane swings sharply right. Continue for about 1/2 mile past farms and houses.

THE GATEHOUSE TO SANDFORD ORCAS MANOR

⑨ At the side of a large barn leave the lane and bear right along a grass and gravel footpath. There is a green sign for the **Macmillan Way** on the signpost. Go through a gate to follow the track as it winds along the valley. When you come to a field keep straight ahead with a fence on your left towards a wood. Bear a little right, cross a stile into the wood and climb the narrow path a little to your left. Go up some steps to join a wide track and keep on uphill.

⑩ When the wide track curves left from a clearing keep straight on up a very narrow path – overgrown but passable – for about 30yds to emerge at the top of the hill by a golf course. Continue along the edge of the golf course, keeping a fence and hedge close on your left, past the club house to a lane.

⑪ Turn right downhill to meet the **Sandford Orcas** road again at point 6. This time turn left down the road for about 1/2 mile to a bridleway sign on the left.

⑫ Turn left, following the direction of the sign up a hedged path, **Quarr Lane**. The path broadens as you gain height. Bear left at a T-junction and soon the track becomes a wide cobbled way descending towards **Sherborne**. As you near the town the track becomes asphalted and leads to a road by **Quarr Lane Park**. Bear right beside the road to meet the B3145. Cross the road in front of the **Mermaid Inn** and walk down the pavement beside the B3145. When you reach the A30 turn right for a few yards, then left opposite the **Antelope Hotel** down **Higher Cheap Street**. Retrace your steps down **Cheap Street** and **South Street**, turning left into **Ludbourne Road** to return to your car.

Date walk completed:

Walk 9

BUCKLAND NEWTON AND THE VALLEY OF THE CERNE

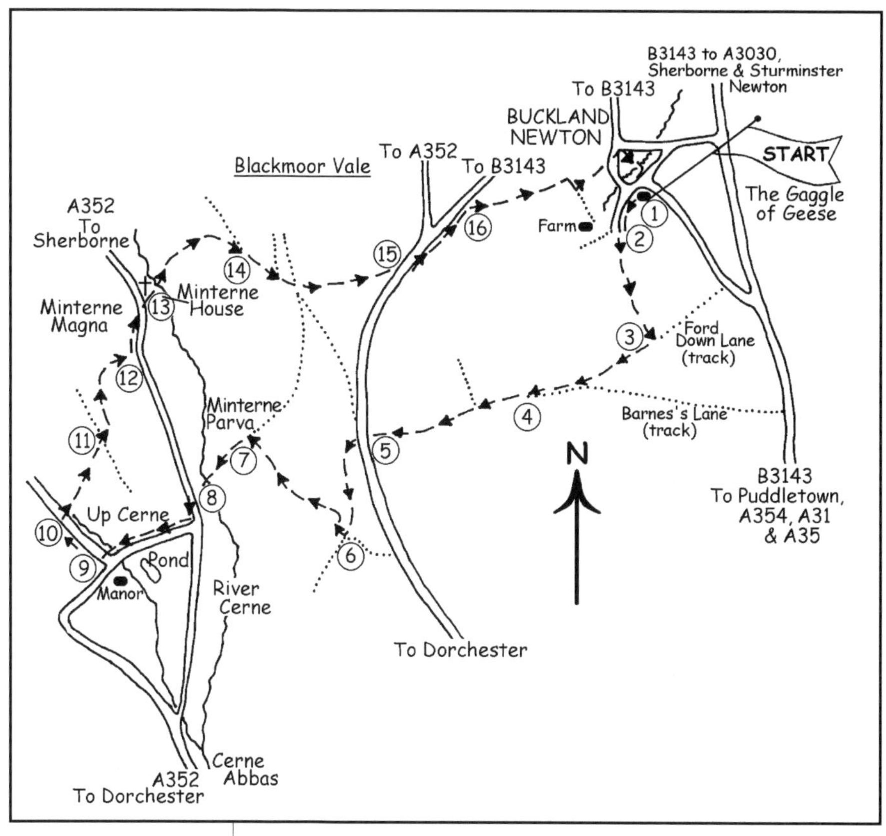

Distance:
8 miles

Starting point:
The Gaggle of Geese pub car park. GR 689050

Map: OS Explorer 117 Cerne Abbas and Bere Regis

How to get there: *Buckland Newton is just west of the B3143 midway between Dorchester and Sherborne. Turn for Buckland Newton off the B3143, drive past the turning for Cranes Meadow on the left and take the next turning on the left. Continue for about 1/4 mile to the pub.*

THATCHED COTTAGES IN UP CERNE

One of Dorset's greatest attractions for the walker is the variety of its scenery. This exciting walk could almost be described as taking place in two worlds! We start from Buckland Newton, a small village cradled in gently curving chalk downland on the southern fringe of the Blackmoor Vale. Hill paths lead high on the downs with magnificent views over the valley of the Cerne. We cross the valley to discover Up Cerne, an attractive village with a fine Elizabethan manor house. After a visit to Minterne Magna, and perhaps a roam round the gardens of Minterne House, we climb the downs again and enjoy a complete change of scene. The chalk escarpment suddenly ceases and we look down on the Blackmoor Vale, once a great forest and still giving that impression with its narrow, winding lanes and small, thickly-hedged fields. This is Thomas Hardy's vale of 'languorous blue mist' and the setting for the later editions of *The Woodlanders*.

Buckland Newton lies close to the source of the river Lydden. It is a peaceful place, scattered around a network of lanes. At its heart you will find the friendliest of Dorset pubs, the delightfully named **Gaggle of Geese**. A large whitewashed house, it once served as the village shop. When it became a pub it was named 'The Royal Oak'. But as a subsequent owner kept geese and customers enjoyed seeing the 'gaggle' the name was changed. The birds still flourish and when we called troops of baby geese were being taught the ways of the world by their proud parents! Auctions of rare poultry are held in May and September each year, raising thousands of pounds for various charities.

The bar area is cool and comfortable and there is a separate restaurant with a charming cottage-like atmosphere. The emphasis is on good, home-cooked food using local produce whenever possible. Excellent steaks are available. A popular dish is the 'Pub Classic', a highly satisfying meal composed of ham, fried eggs, baked beans, sausages and chips. The impressive fish menu included a delicious breaded plaice stuffed with shrimps and mushrooms. Real ales are Badger Best, Ringwood Fortyniner, Ringwood Best and a guest ale.

Opening times *are 12 noon to 2.30 pm and 6.30 pm to 11 pm. Meals are served from 12 noon to 2 pm and 6.30 pm to 10 pm. If you intend a group visit order your meal beforehand so that it can be ready for you when you return.*
Telephone: 01300 345249/345157.

The Walk

① From the car park entrance turn left up the road. Just past the telephone box turn left along a lane signed 'No Through Road'. After about 1/4 mile you pass **Knap Farm** and a joining lane on the right.

② Keep straight ahead up the concrete lane. After passing a large farm building the way becomes a grassy track and leads through a gate. Walk up the side of the meadow ahead with a hedge on your left. Beware the ankle-twisting entrances to a large badger sett! The meadow dips to a gate opening to **Ford Down Lane**, a stony track.

③ Turn right up the track to a gate leading to a meadow. The ground rises ahead and there is no clear path. The angle of the blue arrow bridleway sign is misleading so you need to navigate carefully. Ignore the angle of the sign, go through the gate and bear very slightly right to walk up the meadow to the hedge on the other side. At the hedge, bear right, with the hedge on your left, to a gate on your left.

④ Go through the gate and turn right to follow a wide grassy track bordered with ferns and flowers. This is **Barnes's Lane**, named after a 17th-century ancestor of Dorset's famous poet commemorated in **Buckland Newton** church. Continue for a little over a mile to a road.

⑤ Cross the road and go through two small gates. Again you need to navigate carefully as our path is not clear for the first few yards. Ignore a narrow track leading left and another on your right and walk straight ahead down the grassy hillside, keeping the trees on your left. Soon the path becomes clear, leading downhill through a wood, then along the crest of the hillside bordering the **Cerne valley**. The trees part to reveal beautiful views over rounded meadows and woodlands. Follow the narrow path along the hillside to a prominent signpost.

⑥ Turn right at the signpost, following the sign for **Minterne Parva** and the **Wessex Ridgeway** symbol. A very narrow path (surprising for a Ridgeway!) leads steeply downhill to a thick line of bushes. **Be careful at this point!** Leave the obvious path, which runs through the bushes to cease in front of a wire fence, and turn right with

THE DELIGHTFULLY NAMED GAGGLE OF GEESE PUB, BUCKLAND NEWTON

the bushes on your left. Continue for about 50yds, where the path becomes clear and turns sharply left down to a gate. Now the path ahead is easy to follow as it continues down a field into the valley and curves right then left to become a good track and bring you to a crosspath.

⑦ Turn left, following the sign 'To Main Road'. Follow the lane past the farms and houses of **Minterne Parva** to the road, the A352.

⑧ Turn left beside the road for about 100yds, then turn right up the quiet lane signed '**Up Cerne**'. The lane dips into a valley and through a row of magnificent beech trees on the left there is a splendid view of the lakes in the grounds of **Up Cerne Manor**. Pass the thatched cottages in **Up Cerne** and cross the stream to meet another lane.

⑨ Turn right along the lane. Over the fields on your left you will see **Up Cerne Manor**. After about $1/4$ mile look for a bridleway on the right.

⑩ Turn right up the grassy track, which becomes more stony as it climbs the hillside through woods. In a little under $1/2$ mile, as you near the top, the path swings left. Look carefully for a narrow path on the right with bridleway signs.

⑪ Turn right through the hedge and follow the grassy path straight ahead downhill (a short local diversion). The path curves left to a gate. You are now back on the map again. Through the gate follow the direction of the arrow and bear half-right diagonally down the field. Go through a wide gap and continue past a small chalk quarry on your left. A clear track leads down the slope and swings right through a gate. Follow the avenue of fine trees ahead to the main road, the A352.

⑫ Turn left to walk through **Minterne Magna**. You pass the entrance to **Minterne House Gardens** on your right.

The gardens are open to the public daily from March to November. They are noted for their waterfalls and cascades and brilliant displays of rhododendrons and magnolias. In the 17th century the house was the home of the first Sir Winston Churchill. Later it became the property of the Digby family, who landscaped the grounds in the style of 'Capability' Brown.

⑬ Just past the entrance turn right along a wide track, passing the church on your left. Cross the stream and go through a gate. The track rises beside fences on the left to a signpost. Keep ahead uphill following the sign '**Bridleway to**

Buckland' through a gate and up a field. At the top the path bears a little right through another gate. From the gate bear half-right up the grass and go through a gate in a wire fence. Bear half-left across the hillside to the hedge at the top and with the hedge on your left continue to a gate on your left opening to a track running along the crest of the ridge.

⑭ Turn right and follow this wide way for almost a mile with views over the **Blackmoor Vale** on your left and the **Cerne valley** on your right.

⑮ When you reach the road turn left beside it for about 100yds then take the lane on the right signed for **Buckland Newton**. Far below the **Blackmoor Vale** stretches northwards with **Dungeon Hill** rising, in Hardy's words, 'out of the level like a great whale'.

⑯ After about 100yds turn right over a cattle grid and follow the tarmac track as it curves along the hillside. **Buckland Newton** is settled comfortably in the valley. Follow the track as it swings right past a bridleway sign on the left. After about 50yds turn left at the next bridleway sign, through a gate. Keep ahead over a field and past a row of attractive cottages to a lane. Bear left up the lane to the church and turn right through the churchyard. Among the church's many interesting features is a little winding stair leading to a Priest's Room above the south porch. From the south porch bear a little left down the grass and follow the hedged footpath running downhill beside the vicarage garden. Cross the **Lydden stream**, go through a gate and walk up the field ahead to go through another gate to a lane. Turn right down the lane to the **Gaggle of Geese** and your car.

Date walk completed:

Walk 10

OSMINGTON MILLS AND WHITE NOTHE

THE SUPERB VIEW FROM THE CLIFFTOP ABOVE OSMINGTON MILLS

Distance:
8½ miles

Starting point:
The inn car park. GR 737818

Map: OS Outdoor Leisure 15 Purbeck and South Dorset (East and West sheet)

How to get there: *Osmington Mills is on the coast about 2½ miles east of Weymouth. Take the A353 Weymouth to Warmwell road, then beside Osmington Garage turn down the small road signed to Osmington Mills. Continue for about ¾ mile to the Smugglers Inn car park, signed on the right overlooking the sea. The inn is in the valley opposite.*

This is a splendid walk. We follow the Dorset Coast Path for about five miles, from Osmington Mills, a tiny hamlet tucked into a steep-sided ravine, past Ringstead with its tales of pirates and smugglers, to White Nothe, a huge wall of chalk marking the westernmost point of the Purbeck coast. There is magnificent scenery to enjoy and a wealth of wildlife. Our return route takes a higher path, giving views inland over beautiful rolling downs. Owing to a landslip part of our route is diverted through attractive woodland.

During the 18th century the beach at Osmington Mills made the ideal landing place for cargoes of contraband goods brought from the Continent. The King of the Smugglers, Pierre Latour, or 'French Peter' as he was known in the trade, made his headquarters in the pub where we begin this walk. As you might expect, it is called the **Smugglers Inn**. Set snugly in a hollow protected from the sea, the pub has welcomed travellers since the 13th century. Smoke-blackened fireplaces, low beamed ceilings and stout wooden tables and chairs contribute to its relaxing old world atmosphere. Families have their own room and restaurant area.

The Smugglers is famous for its locally caught lobster and seafood platters. Summer salads include Scottish smoked salmon with prawns and chive cream cheese, dressed crab and home-cooked ham and peach. Among more substantial meals on offer we were tempted by steak and kidney pie cooked in Dorset ale and Beef Stifadho, a traditional Greek dish of braised beef, shallots and tomatoes cooked in red wine with herbs. Real ales are Courage Best, Ruddles County, Wadworth 6X and Ringwood Old Thumper and there is a wine list of over 40 wines.

Dogs are welcome on leads in the garden and there is a children's play area.

Opening times *are from 11 am to 11 pm in summer and from 11 am to 2.30 pm and 6.30 pm to 11 pm in winter. The inn offers accommodation – book early! Telephone: 01305 833125.*

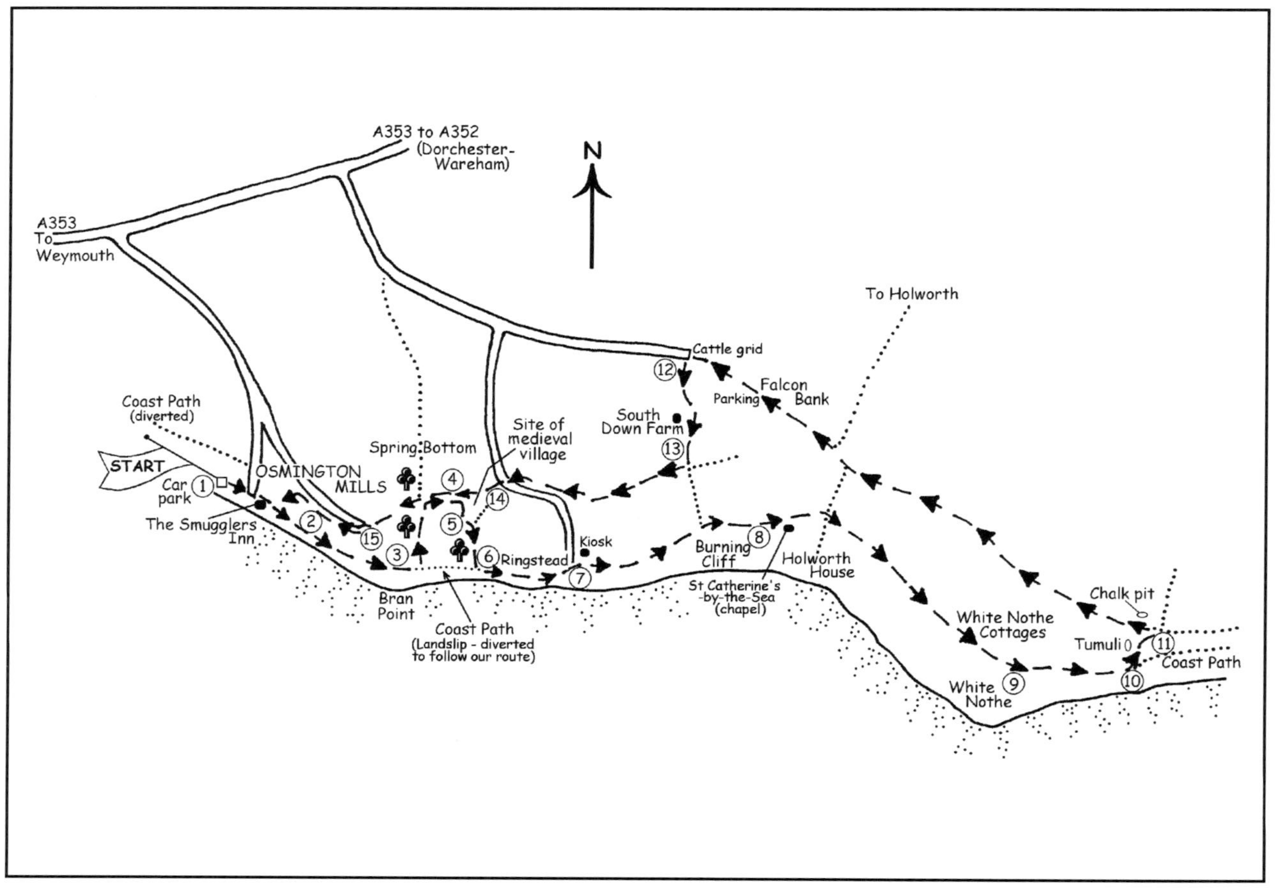
A353 to A352
(Dorchester-
Wareham)
N
A353
To
Weymouth
To Holworth
Cattle grid
Falcon
Bank
Parking
Coast Path
(diverted)
START
Car
park
The Smugglers
Inn
OSMINGTON
MILLS
Spring Bottom
Site of
medieval
village
South
Down Farm
Kiosk
Ringstead
Burning
Cliff
Holworth
House
St Catherine's
-by-the-Sea
(chapel)
Bran
Point
Coast Path
(Landslip - diverted
to follow our route)
White Nothe
Cottages
Chalk pit
Tumuli
Coast Path
White
Nothe

The Walk

① Follow the footpath sign '**Coast Path Ringstead, Lulworth Cove**' and go down the steps to the front of the **Smugglers Inn**. Turn left round the thatched part of the inn, then bear right following the **Coast Path** sign. Go through a small wooden gate and walk up the cliff to go through an identical gate. Continue uphill towards the top of the cliff. Now you have a superb view over **Weymouth Bay** to **Portland**, a dark shape on the horizon. Below, waves cream along the edges of inaccessible beaches and ahead rises the massive 500ft headland of **White Nothe**.

② Steps lead to the top of the cliff through a wooded area then the path follows the clifftop past two concrete pill boxes.

③ After about 1/2 mile you come to a barrier at **Bran Point**. The path is diverted here owing to a landslip. Turn left, following the diversion sign – a large white D. Cross a stile, go over a track and cross another stile. The path runs gently uphill through bushes then winds through woodland to become a broad track. Over a bridge you come to a crosstrack. Turn right and continue to a footpath sign.

④ Turn right, signed '**To Coast Path**'. After about 50yds look over a gate to the meadow on your left. This is the site of the medieval village of **East Ringstead**, believed to have been destroyed by pirates. Some grassed-over embankments are all that remain today. The track descends seawards.

⑤ After about 1/4 mile turn left following the sign for the **Coast Path**. After crossing a dip the path bears a little left down steps then curves right to continue downhill through woods. Just after crossing a brick and concrete bridge follow the path right along the left hand bank of the stream downhill. When you reach the original **Coast Path** turn left up some steps.

⑥ Continue through bushes and over wooden footbridges to **Ringstead village**. Bear slightly right to continue heading east with houses on your left. On your right a path leads down to the beach where there is often a good chance of finding fossils. In the past you might have spotted smugglers at work as this was a favoured landing spot. They used a thatched cottage on the shore as their headquarters. Continue along the track which curves left and becomes an asphalt lane.

⑦ Just before you come to a kiosk on the right (teas, ice-creams, home-made cakes, fish and chips) turn right by a marker stone for **White Nothe**, passing toilets on your left. Follow the signs for White Nothe over stiles and across footbridges. Climb some steps to emerge on the clifftop once more. You are now on the top of **Burning Cliff**. Below is a huge landslip of vertical boulders and crumbling earth covering 115 acres.

Burning Cliff derives its name from the years between 1826 and 1830 when it burned almost continuously owing to the oxidisation of oil-bearing shale in its surface. Thomas Hardy suggests a different reason for the cliff's name in his short story about smugglers, 'The Distracted Preacher'. The heroine, knowing Customs officers are on watch, sets a gorse bush alight to 'warn off' an approaching ship full of contraband.

⑧ Continue along the grassy path and climb steps to meet an asphalt track. Follow this past a house on the right. Now look carefully for a sign on the right for a tiny chapel, **St Catherine's-by-the-Sea**. Turn right for a few yards, then go through the gate on the left into the chapel. Above the altar are three beautiful engraved glass windows. Return to the track to resume your former heading. A few yards further on leave the track and cross a stile, following the sign for **White Nothe**. The narrow path leads past a house on the right. Cross the track leading to **Holworth House** and go over a stile. Ahead you will see the cottages on the top of **White Nothe** so keep to the path over stiles as it leads you to them.

⑨ Pass the cottages on your left, following the sign for **Lulworth Cove**. A magnificent view eastward stretches before you, far over the natural arch of **Bat's Hole** and **Swyre Head** to the tip of **St Aldhelm's Head**.

⑩ After about $^1/_2$ mile look carefully for a stile on the left and a marker stone for **Daggers Gate**. Turn left over the stile and walk up the field ahead with a fence on your left, passing two Bronze Age burial mounds, towards a gate and stile.

⑪ Just **before** the gate turn left, with a fence on your right (almost doubling back on your former track), to follow a path beside a field. The burial mounds are on your left and a small chalk pit on your right. Continue through a gate signed for **South Down** and **Ringstead**. Bear a little right downhill over a stile to pass a thatched barn on your left. Over a stile you join a white track. Follow this straight on uphill, signed '**National Trust South Down**'. After about 100yds when the track curves right keep straight ahead through a gate. The path levels as you go through the next gate and now runs high along the crest of the down. Continue over stiles and across the parking area at **Falcon Bank**.

⑫ Just before you come to the cattle grid at the end of the parking area turn left down a white track with a prominent notice 'No Cars – footpath only to the sea'. Follow the track downhill and round **South Down Farm**, passing all buildings on your right. Go through a gate and follow the track slightly uphill for about 150yds.

⑬ At this point the track swings left. Turn right over a stile (no sign) and keep straight ahead along the crest of a ridge with a fence on your left. Follow the line of the fence as it curves right into the valley, then bear left, with a hedge on your right, to cross a footbridge and stile. Walk up the field ahead and cross the stile to a lane. Turn right a little uphill.

⑭ After about 50yds, where the lane curves right, turn left through a gateway (no sign) to pass a bungalow on the left. As you enter woodland, pass a track on the left and turn right through a gate. Follow the broad track ahead signed '**Upton and Osmington Mills**'. (You are retracing part of our earlier route.) Follow the next sign for **Osmington Mills** to leave our earlier path and keep straight ahead through a gate to cross a stream in an attractive woodland glade, **Spring Bottom**. Bear a little left up the bank ahead and follow the grassy path around the hillside to cross a stile. Turn right past a thatched cottage on the right to a lane.

⑮ Bear right down the lane towards **Osmington Mills**. When you come to an iron field gate on the left, turn left over the stile beside it and walk down the meadow just to the left of a white house to rejoin the **Coast Path**. Turn right to retrace your route for a few yards past the **Smugglers Inn** to the car park.

Date walk completed:

Walk 11

ANSTY AND THE DORSETSHIRE GAP

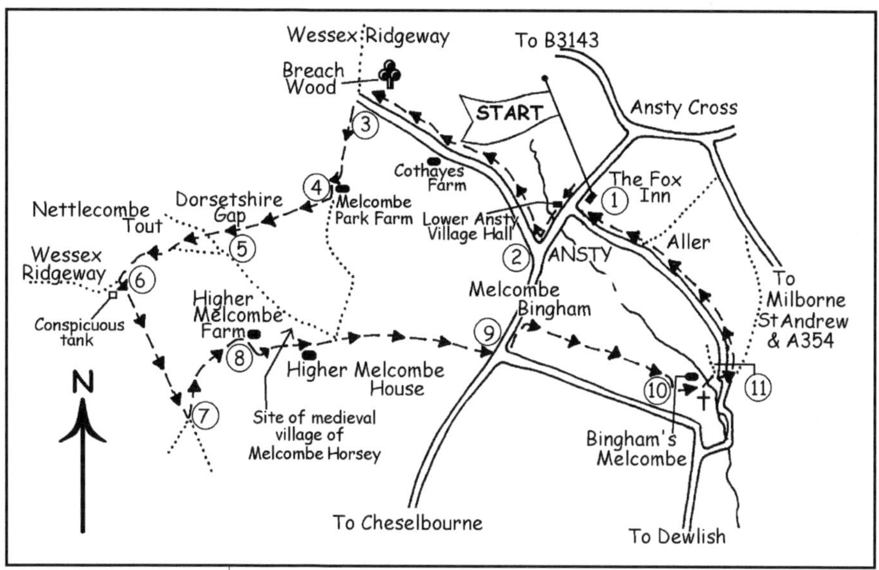

Distance:
7 miles

Starting point:
The Fox Inn car park, or beside the village hall just past the pub on the right.
GR 767033

Map: OS Explorer 117 Cerne Abbas and Bere Regis

How to get there: *The best approach is via the A354 Blandford Forum-Dorchester road. Turn off the A354 in Milborne St Andrew, following the sign for Ansty and Milton Abbas. (There is a brown sign for the Fox Inn also.) Continue for about 2 miles then turn left for Ansty. After about 4 miles turn left again at Ansty Cross, following the sign for Melcombe Bingham. The Fox Inn is about 1/2 mile down the lane on the left.*

Dorset has many magical places in store for the walker and one of the most thrilling must be the Dorsetshire Gap, a narrow cleft cutting through the high northern downs linking the chalk river valleys with the Blackmoor Vale. For centuries travellers have used this pass. Today we can walk in their footsteps and find few changes. The steep slopes of Nettlecombe Tout dominate the pass to the west. The downs east of the pass remain untouched by the plough, brilliant with cowslips and orchids in early summer. From Ansty, a group of scattered settlements at the foot of the downs, the route follows part of the historic Wessex Ridgeway to the Gap then returns past the site of the deserted medieval village at Melcombe Horsey and a fine manor house in glorious surroundings at Bingham's Melcombe. (Not to be confused with Melcombe Bingham!) Make certain you choose a clear day for this walk as there are stunning views in all directions.

The houses and farms of Ansty spread across the countryside. Apart from Ansty proper there is Pleck or Little Ansty, Higher Ansty and Lower Ansty. To find one of the best pubs in Dorset, the **Fox Inn**, you must seek out Lower Ansty. Fortunately the route to the inn is well signed! There is a warm welcome for everyone in this charming 200-year-old country house hotel. Until 1915 it was the family home of Charles Hall – who founded the well-known brewery here in 1777. When we arrived, dusty after our walk, we were delighted to see at the entrance to the Fox Inn's Ansty Bar a large notice proclaiming 'Walkers Welcome!' Inside, the atmosphere was warm and friendly. You could choose from a wide range of snacks and a comprehensive menu. Steak and ale pies and mixed grills are popular and lighter meals include Wessex pasties and baked potato skins with a variety of fillings. A carvery is served in the lounge bar and à la carte dishes in the Woodhouse restaurant. Real ales include Tanglefoot and Badger Best, cider is Blackthorn and there is a well balanced and extensive wine list. Children and dogs are welcome and there is a large garden. Accommodation includes 14 tastefully decorated bedrooms and a bunkhouse with all facilities.

The inn is open *every day from 11 am to 11 pm and meals are served from 11 am to 3 pm and 7 pm to 10 pm.*
Telephone: 01258 880328.

The Walk

① Turn left from the front of the **Fox Inn** to walk down the lane passing the **Old Brewery** building, now the village hall, on your right. Lower down the hill you pass the picturesque pottery and cross the **Devil's Brook**. At this point the stream is called **Mash Water** as it was once the drain from the brewery.

② As you come to the first houses in **Melcombe Bingham**, turn right opposite the village sign, following the direction for **Melcombe Park Farm**. Continue along this pleasant lane for about a mile. On your right the houses of Ansty nestle among meadows and woodland in the shadow of **Bulbarrow Hill**. Pass the beautiful gardens of **Cothayes Farm** and follow the lane along the fringe of **Breach Wood**.

③ You meet a crossing track, the **Wessex Ridgeway**, in front of a large barn. Turn left uphill to **Melcombe Park Farm**. Opposite the farmhouse bear right for a few yards then left to walk up the farmyard. Keep ahead to go through the furthest right of three gates.

④ The route seems improbable at this stage as we could see no clear path. But turn immediately right following the sign '**Dorset Gap**'. Walk along the side of a rising meadow with woods on your right and go through a small iron gate.

BINGHAM'S MELCOMBE LAKE

Keep ahead now towards **Nettlecombe Tout**, following the crest of a high ridge with magnificent views north over the **Blackmoor Vale** and south over the downs as far as the coastal hills. At the end of the ridge the ground drops away steeply to a gate a little to your left. Through the gate you arrive at the meeting of several ways at the highest point of the **Dorsetshire Gap**.

⑤ Sign the Visitors Book in a small green box on your right and walk across the **Gap** to a prominent signpost. Bear left to take the terraced path signed for **Folly**, which rises gently between sheer grassy banks bordered by woods around the southern slopes of **Nettlecombe Tout**. The path curves left then a little right past a bridleway leading downhill on the left. Keep your height to go through a gate to leave the wood and follow a clear track up a meadow and through another gate. Keep straight on across the next field until you come to a conspicuous tank on a large concrete support. Here we leave the Ridgeway.

⑥ Turn left (very narrow path), passing the tank on your right, and continue with a hedge on your left. Go through a gate and keep ahead, following a wide track downhill. This open downland is home for roe deer. On your right you pass the embankments of cross dykes possibly prehistoric in origin.

⑦ In a little over ½ mile, just before the next gate, look for a rather battered gate on your left. Turn left through the gate and another gate a few yards further on

THE WELCOMING FOX INN AT ANSTY

(heading north-east) and keep ahead close to a fence on your left for about 30yds. Now take the good path curving right down the hillside towards **Higher Melcombe Farm**.

⑧ Do not go through the gate into the farmyard but turn right just before it through a small gate and follow the field side with a hedge on your left. Go through the next gate and turn left to walk up to the track to meet the lane from the farm. Turn right to follow the lane. The fields on your left are patterned with the embanked outlines of the house plots of **Melcombe Horsey medieval village**. The lane runs past 17th-century **Higher Melcombe House** and **Chapel**.

The house is open May to August by written application to 'The Owner, Higher Melcombe House, Dorchester DT2 7PB'.

Follow the lane to the crossroads just south of **Melcombe Bingham**.

⑨ Turn left for about 200yds then turn right between the houses, following the sign for **Bingham's Melcombe**. Go through a gate and follow the narrow path straight ahead across a field towards a finger of woodland. With the wood on your right continue along the same heading. At the end of the field as the path begins to curve left cross some wooden bars a little to your right, go through a belt of trees and keep straight on over the next field. Ahead you will see **Bingham's Melcombe manor house** at the foot of the wooded hillside. Cross a stile and go through the trees to the smooth green lawn beside the wall of the manor garden. An enormous yew hedge, said to be the tallest in England, towers above the wall.

⑩ Bear right and follow the track as it shortly curves left past the manor and imposing gatehouse. The church and little school are on your right. Once there was a village in this enchanting valley. Cross the footbridge over the **Devil's Brook** where it plunges over a small weir fed by a lake and go round a wooden barrier. Take the path on the left with a fence on the left to cross the grass towards a stile. Do not cross the stile but bear right past a gate and round a wooden barrier to meet a lane.

⑪ Turn left to follow this pleasant lane for a little over a mile, bearing left in the attractive hamlet of **Aller** to meet the road in **Lower Ansty** opposite the village hall. Turn right for the **Fox Inn**.

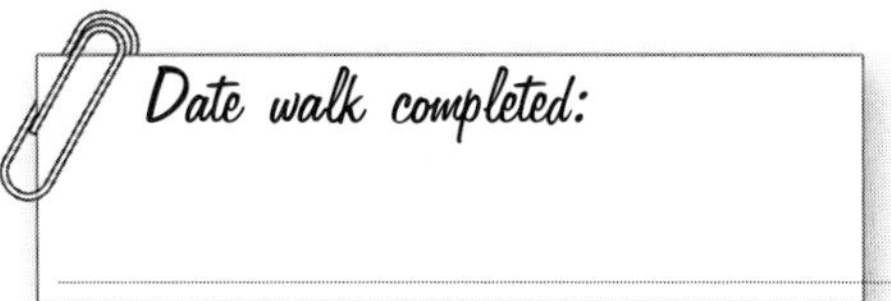

Walk 12

STURMINSTER NEWTON – A STOURSIDE WALK IN THE BLACKMOOR VALE

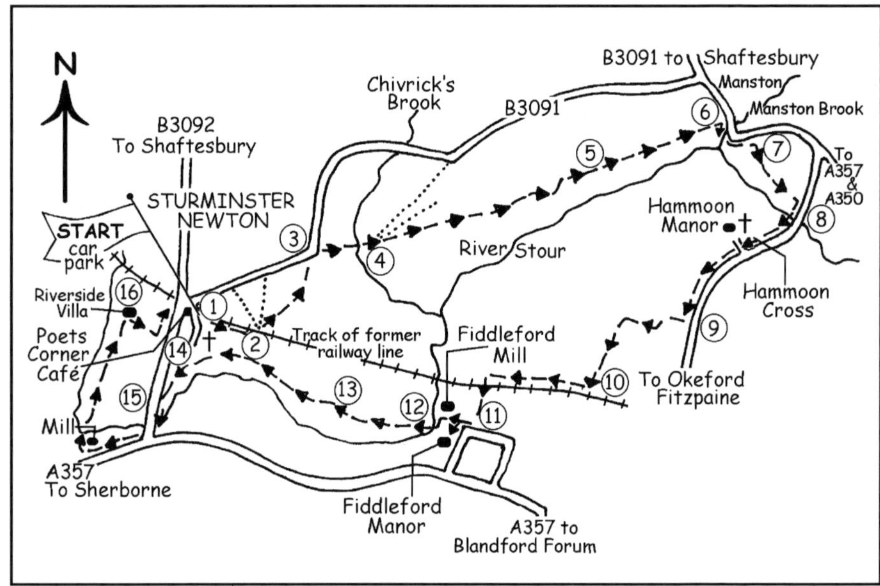

Distance:
7 miles

Starting point:
The long-stay car park detailed right. GR 787142

Map: OS Explorer 129 Yeovil and Sherborne

How to get there: *Turn for Sturminster Newton off the A357 Blandford-Wincanton road along the B3092. Cross the bridge over the Stour, drive through the Market Place and turn right down Station Road for a few yards then turn right for the car park. The entrance is on your left.*

THE MILL BY THE STOUR IN STURMINSTER NEWTON

A few miles north of Blandford Forum the chalk hills of central Dorset give way to the lush pastures of the Blackmoor Vale. It is an idyllic countryside of low hills, thick hedgerows and sunken lanes. Dorset's greatest river, the Stour, winds lazily through the meadows bordered with wild flowers. We begin this walk in one of the county's most attractive market towns, Sturminster Newton, set high on a cliff overlooking the river. Sturminster is an artist's delight! No two houses are alike and they form a fascinating jumble of medieval gables, coaching inns and pretty Georgian cottages. The thatched market house stands in a small square beside the octagonal steps of an ancient cross. From the town we follow the river to Manston and Hammoon, a tiny place with the remains of a 14th-century stone cross, a 700-year-old church and magnificent thatched manor house. We cross the Stour past the mill at Fiddleford and visit one of the earliest manor houses in Dorset, dating from the 1370s. Riverside paths pass a working water mill as they lead back to Sturminster.

The charm of this riverside town and the lovely countryside surrounding it inspired the work of three poets, Thomas Hardy, William Barnes and his friend Robert Young. So I feel fully justified in suggesting that you call in at one of my favourite places for a meal, not a pub this time but the **Poets Corner Café**, directly opposite the large central car park where we begin our walk. The café is ideal for walkers, with a comfortable, homely atmosphere and tasty well-prepared food. A full English breakfast is available all day, home-made soup comes with crusty rolls, there is a range of pasta dishes – try their garlic, onion and prawn in a rich tomato sauce – and some delicious cakes. Particularly tempting is their blueberry and lemon muffin cake. And if you fancy something different, the café has a Turkish theme and offers genuine home-made Turkish musakka, baklava served with clotted cream and real Turkish delight.

Open *every day except Sunday from 9 am to 5 pm.*
Telephone: 01258 473723.

① Leave the car park taking the footpath to the right of Buy-Low's supermarket, signed for **Fiddleford Manor** and **Mill**. The town is soon left behind and ahead there is a fine view of the Iron Age hill fort crowning **Hambledon Hill**.

You are following the route of the former single track Somerset and Dorset Joint Railway closed in 1966. It ran between Bournemouth and Bath with connections at Templecombe for Exeter and London. The car park has taken the place of the station and the supermarket stands on the site of the goods sidings. The wooded banks are rich in wildlife.

② After about $\frac{1}{4}$ mile descend a flight of steps on the left and go through a small wooden gate. Take the right hand path of the three possible paths ahead (it appears to be unsigned by the finger post). This leads across a meadow and over a stile. Bear half-left diagonally over the next meadow and cross the stile. The path now runs between hedges to a lane. Cross straight over and follow the narrow path ahead signed for **Manston Road**. (Do not turn left.) This takes you to the main road, the B3091.

③ Turn right to the corner of the road then keep ahead following the footpath sign for **Manston** and cross a stile. A grassy path leads downhill through gates. Continue down the meadow to cross a footbridge with stiles over **Chivrick's Brook**. (The way is indistinct over the meadows but it is signed.) Keep ahead with a hedge on the left for about 50 yards to a finger post with three signs.

④ Follow the sign for **Manston church** and walk half-right diagonally over the meadow as indicated; go over a stile and narrow concrete footbridge. Continue with a hedge on your right and after about 200yds bear a little left towards the left hand side of a hedge directly ahead. Now you have a beautiful view of the **Stour**. Walk down to the river bank and bear left. The path curves left with a hedge on the right to take you over a concrete bridge and with a stile either end. Cross, and bear left over the meadow with the river on your right. These quiet stretches of the river are a haven for wildlife, including herons and kingfishers.

⑤ Continue over the next concrete bridge by a footpath marker post and keep straight ahead towards a gate. Across the river on your right there is a glimpse of the tower of **Manston church** and **Manston manor**. Follow a clear track over the last meadow, leading to the left of a stone barn with the garden of a bungalow on your right, to the road.

AN IDEAL STOP FOR REFRESHMENTS IN STURMINSTER NEWTON

⑥ Turn right and cross the bridge over the **Manston Brook**. Pass the entrance to the manor and turn right following the sign for **Hammoon** and **Child Okeford**, to face a field. The path has been diverted and differs for a short distance from the OS map. Do not enter the field but turn left, as the marker arrow indicates, to a stile on the right on the corner of the field.

⑦ Turn right over the stile and continue along the edge of the field with a fence then hedges on the left and cross the next stile. (You are now back on the route marked on the OS map.) Keep ahead over the meadow and cross a footbridge with stiles to a lane.

⑧ Turn right and follow the lane to the cross in **Hammoon**. Turn right to see the church and manor then return to the cross and, leaving it on your right, continue along the lane to a bridleway signed for **Fiddleford** on the right.

⑨ Turn right along the gravel track, which turns left then right to a finger post. Turn left through a gate and keep ahead with a hedge on the left to go through another gate and over a footbridge. One hundred yards further on you rejoin the railway track.

⑩ Turn right and follow the bridleway sign until you come to a crosspath. Turn left down the track to a lane.

⑪ Turn right and cross the stream to face the approach to **Fiddleford Mill**. A visit to **Fiddleford Manor** is a 'must'! So bear left here then right over the car park and follow the grassy track ahead to the manor.

Fiddleford Manor is administered by English Heritage. Although unfurnished it is a splendid building with beautiful timber roofs to the hall and solar. Entry is free and the manor is open 10 am to 6 pm April to September, 10 am to 4 pm October to March.

Retrace your steps to **Fiddleford Mill** and pass to the left of it. Turn left to cross the footbridges over the mill race and weir.

⑫ Go through a gate, and follow the meadow path signed for **Sturminster Newton** with the river over the grass on your left. This was the countryside William Barnes loved. He celebrated the beauty of his 'cloty' Stour and the simple lives of the people of the **Blackmoor Vale** in his poems. His 'clote', a yellow water lily, still carpets the shallows. Cross a bridge with stiles and bear half-right over the meadow ahead.

⑬ Go through a gap and keep

ahead, with a hedge on the right, to a stile on the right. Cross and follow the clear path bearing a little left to a gate. Go through and follow the track signed '**Penny Street**' to a lane. Turn left, and follow the lane round to the right. Keep straight ahead up a narrow path and go up the steps into the churchyard. The enormous Wellingtonia on your right is over 100ft high! Pass the church (on your right) and walk up the lane ahead. Cross the foot of a road and keep ahead past a charming thatched cottage.

⑭ At the foot of the next road look carefully for a narrow, hedged footpath on the left signed '**Town Bridge via Coach Road**'. Follow this pleasant way to the B3092.

⑮ Turn left and cross **Sturminster's** splendid 15th-century bridge to the A357. Turn right along the pavement and follow the road for a short distance then turn right to walk down to **Sturminster Mill**.

This working water mill dates from the early 17th century. In 1907 the traditional water wheel was replaced by a water turbine. It is open Easter to 30th September, Saturday, Sunday, Monday and Thursday from 11 am to 5 pm. Visits by parties can take place by prior arrangement. Telephone: 01747 854355.

Cross the **Stour** by the weir footbridges. Go through a gate and walk up the meadow ahead. After another gate you continue to the top of a cliff, at the foot of which the **Stour** winds round an island.

⑯ At the top, just before another gate, turn right along the top of the recreation ground. On your left is **Riverside Villa**, where Thomas Hardy spent two happy years, from 1876 to 1878, with his first wife, Emma. While he was there he wrote *The Return of the Native* and several poems about the **Sturminster** countryside. When you come to the road turn left through the **Market Place** then right down **Station Road** past the **Poets Corner Café** to your car.

Date walk completed:

Walk 13

THE IWERNE VALLEY AND ASHMORE WOOD

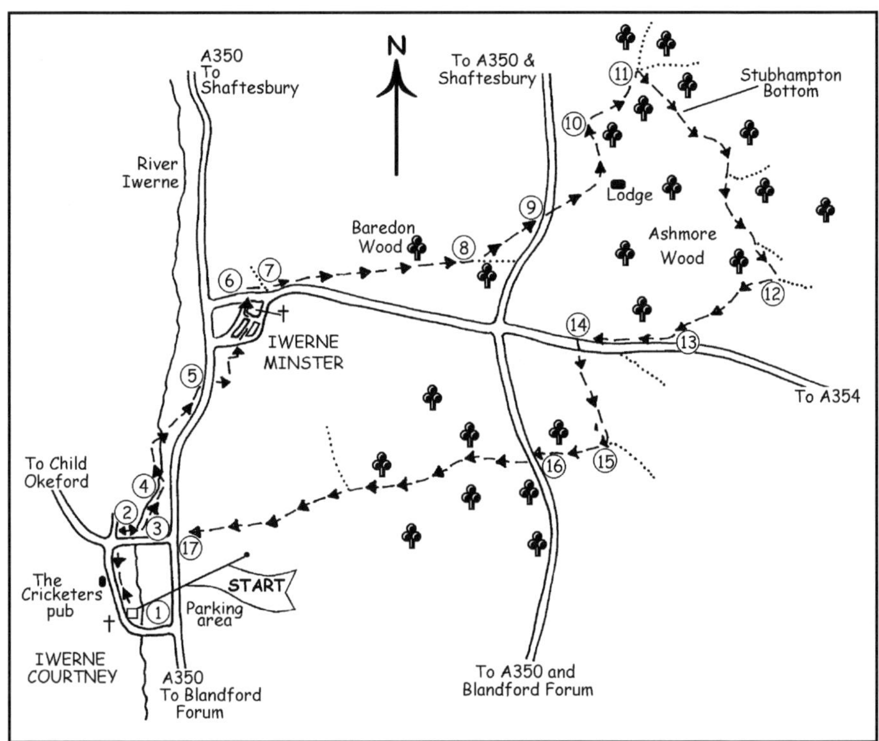

Distance:
9 miles

Starting point:
The parking area described, opposite the church.
GR 860125

Map: OS Explorer 118 Shaftesbury and Cranborne Chase

How to get there: *Iwerne Courtney (also called Shroton) lies just west of the A350 Blandford Forum-Shaftesbury road, about 5 miles north of Blandford Forum. Heading north, turn for Iwerne Courtney and follow the road round a right bend to the church on your left and a large parking area on your right.*

THE ESTATE VILLAGE OF IWERNE MINSTER

The little river Iwerne runs south to meet the Stour, carving a beautiful valley through the western uplands of Cranborne Chase. Settlements dating from Saxon times have grown up beside the river, which has given its name to the two contrasting villages featured in this walk. Iwerne Courtney, our starting point, is an attractive mix of old and new – thatched cottages and neat Georgian houses blend happily with more modern developments. Iwerne Minster still retains some older buildings but essentially it is an estate village rebuilt in brick in the late 19th century in the 'manorial' style reminiscent of Tudor and Elizabethan days.

From the valley the route leads into the rolling hills of the Chase through magnificent woodlands to follow a magical path along a deep glen, which, with its wealth of wild flowers, birds and butterflies, must be one of Dorset's treasures. After you have followed the tree-shaded path which threads this lovely valley you will wonder how it could possibly have come by the unromantic name of Stubhampton Bottom!

The Cricketers pub is situated in the heart of Iwerne Courtney opposite the village green. And, as its name suggests, it is also close to the village's well-maintained cricket pitch. Inside, the cricketing theme is very much in evidence with bats, balls, stumps and cricketing sketches decorating the bar and the walls – even the front door. The atmosphere is pleasant and relaxed and the owner takes pride in welcoming guests and making sure they enjoy their visit. You can eat your meal in the bar or the separate restaurant. As well as the more usual bar snacks the menu offers a wide range of imaginative dishes. When we called these included seafood pancake topped with cheese and a tomato sauce, Moroccan Lamb Tagine with couscous and lamb hock in a red wine and mushroom sauce. Fresh fish is delivered daily straight from the boats. Real ales are Spitfire (from a Kent brewery), Bass, Greene King IPA and Abbot Ale and a guest; you will also find some interesting speciality wines.

Opening times *are from 11.30 am to 2.20 pm (3 pm at weekends) and 6.30 pm to 11.30 pm. Meals are served from 12 noon to 2 pm during the week, until 2.30 pm at weekends. In summer meals are served in the evenings from 6.30 pm to 9 pm, in winter from 7 pm to 9 pm. Book ahead if you plan a group visit. Telephone: 01258 860421.*

① Leaving with the parking area on your right and the church on your left, walk up the road and along the main village street. You pass the **Cricketers** pub and the thatched post office on your left. Continue through the village to the crossroads. On your left on the corner a beautiful cross standing on an ancient Christian base marks the millennium.

② Turn right along **Frog Lane** for about 200yds and look for a stile and footpath sign in the hedge on your left.

③ Turn left over the stile with the tiny **river Iwerne** running beside you on the left. Pick your way through an overgrown patch then continue over the meadow keeping the hedge and stream on your left.

④ After about 400yds you come to a wooden footbridge. Turn left to cross the bridge then bear right beside the meadow, with the stream now on your right, to go through a gate. Follow the tarmac path, leaving several houses on your left. After passing the last house turn left over a stile and walk over the meadow ahead, keeping a fence about 30yds away on your left. Go through a gate and follow the track to a lane. Turn right for about 50yds then turn left to follow a narrow tarmac path leading to an estate. Keep ahead along the footpath and take the first turning on the right to meet the main road, the A350.

⑤ Turn left for a few yards then cross the road and take the footpath signed '**Footpath to Village**'. Tarmac quickly gives way to grass as the path turns left towards the village. The spire of **Iwerne Minster church** – one of the three surviving medieval church spires in Dorset – rises above the trees. The path turns right past the cricket pavilion then left past the children's playground to meet a lane in the village. Turn right for a few yards then bear left up the road to face the church and churchyard. Turn left, with the churchyard on your right, to meet another lane. (Visit this fine church if you have time. It features many different dates and styles; much of the nave and north aisle are Norman, dating from the mid-12th century.)

⑥ Turn right up the lane for about 150yds to a bridleway on your left signed '**Bridleway to Ashmore**' by a sign '**Valley View**'.

⑦ Follow the bridleway through a

THE VILLAGE PUB IN IWERNE MINSTER

gate where the tarmac becomes a grassy, hedged track leading uphill. On your left the hill slopes down to a softly curving wooded valley. Looking back there are wide views over **Blackmoor Vale** dominated by **Hambledon Hill**, its summit ringed by the ramparts of an Iron Age fort. The track climbs under the magnificent beech trees of **Baredon Wood** then traces a more open route to the outskirts of another small wood.

⑧ At the approach to the wood leave the track and follow the bridleway signed on your left. This leads through the wood, bearing half-left to bring you out on the open hillside. There is no clear path but, keeping the same heading, bear half-left up the hillside towards the hedge at the top and go through a small gate to a road.

⑨ Cross the road and follow an elegant tarmac drive bordered by beech trees towards a lodge. Just before the lodge turn left through a small gate signed '**Bridleway to Ashmore**'. Continue beside the meadows with woods on your right, going through a series of small gates. In just over 1/4 mile the path descends to a final gate.

⑩ Go through the gate to a crosstrack. Turn right for only about 50yds then bear left down the edge of the meadow with a hedge on your right. Keep the woods on your right as the path bears left to go through a gate. Follow the path ahead as it descends very steeply to a gate at the foot of the hill.

⑪ Go through the gate to meet a wide gravel track running through **Stubhampton Bottom**. Turn right to follow this enchanted valley described by Treves over 150 years ago as 'a place shut away from the world ... such a glen as belongs to the country of the *Idylls of the King*.' Almost enclosed by steep wooded hillsides it is little changed today. When the gravel track swings left keep straight on along a grassy path. Pass a footpath on your left and keep ahead until you emerge from the woods. At this point the path ahead begins to turn left. Following the signs, leave it and continue along the right hand bridleway for about 300yds.

⑫ On your right you will see a post marked with yellow footpath signs and the symbol of the **Wessex Ridgeway** – a mythical creature known as a Wyvern.

This is the standard of the 43rd (Wessex) Division of the Dorsetshire Regiment and was first carried into battle by King Alfred in the 9th century.

Turn right to follow the **Wessex Ridgeway** steeply uphill through coppice woods brilliant with bluebells in spring. At the top of the hill the woods give way to meadowland on the left. Keep ahead, with woods on your right, through a gate to a road.

⑬ Turn right beside the road and pass a bridleway sign on your left. Continue for about 200yds to a second bridleway sign on your left.

⑭ Turn left to walk through another bluebell wood.

⑮ When the wood ends turn right to walk beside fields, with woods on your right, to meet a road.

⑯ Turn left for a few yards then take the footpath on the right past a gate. A wide white track now leads through beautiful park-like woodland for over a mile. When the woods cease and you have open country on your left continue ahead with a hedge on your right. As the track curves left keep straight on along a grassy path running beside fields with the hedge still on your right. The path descends into the **Iwerne valley** with a splendid view of **Iwerne Courtney** nestling at the foot of the steep slopes of **Hambledon Hill**. Follow the path over stiles to the A350.

⑰ Cross the road and follow the lane directly ahead – **Frog Lane**. Pass the stile on the right, which we climbed outbound. Now retrace your steps, turning left at the crossroads to pass the **Cricketers** pub and return to your car.

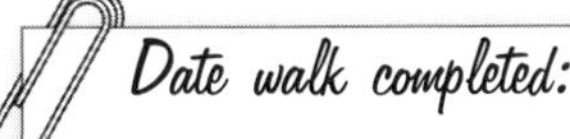

Walk 14

COMPTON ABBAS, FONTMELL DOWN AND MELBURY HILL

MELBURY HILL

Distance:
7 miles

Starting point:
Compton Abbas airfield restaurant car park. GR 890185

Alternative starting point:
As the airfield closes at dusk in winter you may prefer to use the small National Trust car park on nearby Spreadeagle Hill. GR 886187. Turn right from the car park, with the road on your left for about 80yds, cross a stile, turn right, and join the route of the walk at point 2.

Map: OS Explorer 118 Shaftesbury and Cranborne Chase

How to get there: *There is no approach to the airfield from the A350 in Compton Abbas. Approach from the east via the A354 Dorchester-Salisbury road. Turn right, signed for Shaftesbury, along the A350. At the next roundabout turn right. Follow the sign for Compton Abbas airfield and eventually turn off right. After about 100yds turn left into the car park. Approaching from the west, follow the A354 to bypass Blandford, turn left onto the A350, then right as directed above. If you are coming from Shaftesbury take the A30 for Salisbury then turn right onto the B3081. Leave the B3081, following the sign for Melbury Abbas, to the turning on the left for the airfield.*

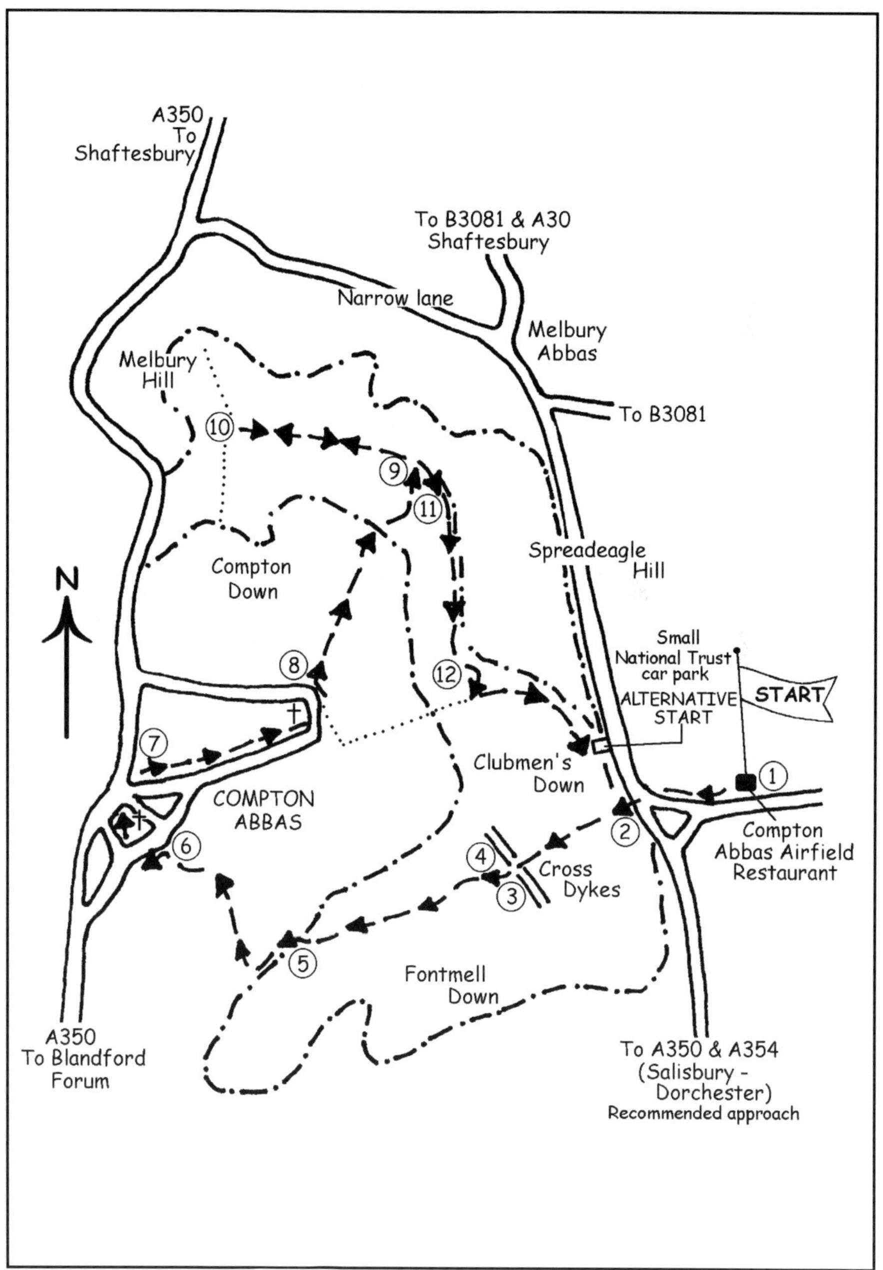
A350
To
Shaftesbury
To B3081 & A30
Shaftesbury
Narrow lane
Melbury
Abbas
Melbury
Hill
To B3081
N
Compton
Down
Spreadeagle
Hill
Small
National Trust
car park
ALTERNATIVE
START
START
Clubmen's
Down
COMPTON
ABBAS
Compton
Abbas Airfield
Restaurant
Cross
Dykes
Fontmell
Down
A350
To Blandford
Forum
To A350 & A354
(Salisbury -
Dorchester)
Recommended approach

This exhilarating walk crosses the Melbury and Fontmell Estate, some of the finest chalk downland in Dorset. The estate was bought by the National Trust in 1977 after a successful public appeal in memory of Thomas Hardy. Today the downs, close cropped by sheep, are a wonderful place for wild flowers, including early purple, pyramidal and bee orchids. Cowslips, kidney and horseshoe vetches and the tiny milkwort are particularly attractive for butterflies and sometimes it is possible to see all the chalkland blues flying at once – the Common, Chalkhill, Adonis and our smallest butterfly, the diminutive Small Blue. Nightingales and willow warblers sing in the woods and at night you will find glow-worms. Areas of scrubland provide sanctuary for roe and fallow deer. The route climbs Melbury Hill to reward you with one of Dorset's most magnificent views.

Compton Abbas Airfield Restaurant, sited on the crest of the downs at 800ft above sea level, is the perfect place to start your walk. The welcome is warm and friendly, there are splendid views, and the food and drink are excellent. When we called, the varied menu included a hearty liver and bacon casserole and chicken breast cooked in cider. Among a wide range of bar snacks we spotted Dorset ham and Stilton and tomato baguettes. The sweets menu included Dorset apple pudding with Calvados sauce. There is a special 'Junior Pilots' menu for children. Ales on offer include Hofbrau Export and Whitbread Bitter.

While you enjoy your meal you are surrounded by all things to do with aviation. The aircraft you will see taking off and landing are mostly Cessnas and Pipers used for training purposes. You can even take a flight yourself! There is a large car park but in winter it is wise to check closing times.

The licensed bar and restaurant are open *every day, 9 am to sunset, breakfast is served from 9.30 am until 12 noon, lunches from 12 noon to 2.30 pm. Teas are available in the afternoon.*
Telephone: 01747 811767.

① Turn right from the airfield car park and when the lane divides continue along the right hand lane to return to the road. Cross the road and go over the stile ahead by the footpath sign to the open downland.

② Walk straight ahead, with a fence on your right, along the crest of the down. A beautiful valley opens on your left.

You are walking in the footsteps of the Clubmen, a band of Dorset men who met on this hill to protest against the devastation caused by the armies on both sides in the Civil War. They took their name from the weapons they carried and later 'club' came to mean any group meeting with a common interest or purpose. Their protest ended when, after a last stand on Hambledon Hill, they were defeated by a detachment of Oliver Cromwell's dragoons.

③ The path dips over **Cross Dykes**, which possibly date from around 500BC, at the beginning of the Iron Age, and could mark a territorial boundary. You are now on **Fontmell Down**. As this is all National Trust

THE RESTAURANT AT COMPTON ABBAS AIRFIELD

land you can wander at will and you may like to explore the down further before continuing with the route of the walk.

④ To continue with the walk from **Cross Dykes** follow the direction of the sign to bear a little right to a stile. Cross and turn left, with a fence on your left, along a green path sloping gently down the hillside. Now you have a glorious view north over the valley sheltering **Compton Abbas** village to the sweeping curve of **Spreadeagle Hill** and the crest of **Melbury Down**. The path leads more steeply downhill through a gate.

⑤ Keep straight ahead through the trees and continue along the top of a field to a fence. Turn right, with the fence on your left, down a field, through more gates. The path now leads slightly downhill to go through a small iron gate. Follow the path, sunk between the roots of great oak trees and carpeted with bluebells in spring, as it winds its way over a stream and past a lake on the right to meet a lane in **Compton Abbas**.

⑥ Turn left along the lane. When it swings left leave the lane and turn right past some garages up a narrow tree-shaded path to the church. Climb the steps to a lane. Continue past the church to the A350. Follow the footpath to the right of the road for a few yards, then go through a gate on your right to the grounds of the old school. (You are not trespassing!) Bear left along the stepping stones then through a wood and down steps to the lane to **East Compton**.

⑦ Turn right along this pleasant, flower-bordered lane passing the **Old Forge** on your left. (Ignore the lane leading sharp right back towards the church.) You are now heading east towards **Spreadeagle Hill**. The lane passes the attractive houses of the old village, many thatched and built of Shaftesbury stone, which matures to a soft grey-green.

This settlement was the original Compton. The name is derived from Saxon 'cumb' and 'tun' meaning 'farm in the valley'. In AD 995 'Abbas' was added to the name of the village when the rich land hereabouts was granted to the Abbey at Shaftesbury.

The lane curves left past a 15th-century tower standing isolated in the middle of a field – all that remains of the earlier church. In 1640 the rector was Thomas Bravell, the leader of the Clubmen. If you look over the churchyard wall in front of the tower you will see the worn steps of an ancient preaching cross. The lane curves right then left again to a wide track on the right marked with a finger post signed for **Melbury Abbas**.

⑧ Turn right along the track with **Spreadeagle Hill** directly ahead, passing an iron gate on your left. Do not go through it but keep ahead with a fence on your left. At the foot of the down go through a gate and a few yards further on turn right through another gate and follow the path, climbing the side of the down, golden with cowslips in spring. Keep the same heading when you meet a wider path and ignoring all other footpath signs continue uphill to a fence.

⑨ Turn left and, with the fence on your right, follow the path to climb **Melbury Hill**. A trig point on the summit marks the site of the former Armada beacon. Pause to enjoy the wonderful view west over the **Blackmoor Vale** to **Sturminster Newton**, **Sherborne** and the plains of the **Stour**, north to **Shaftesbury** on its hilltop, and south over the high downs fringing the vale. On a clear day you can see the radio masts on the top of **Bulbarrow**. Rising to 898ft, **Bulbarrow** is one of Dorset's highest hills.

⑩ Retrace your steps to point 9 and this time keep straight ahead, fence on left, uphill to a gate.

⑪ Turn right just before the gate to walk along the top of **Compton Down** with a fence on your left. This hillside is purple with violets in spring and later yellow with rock roses and vetches. Follow the fence round to the left for about 50yds then look downhill for a stile in the hedge at the foot.

⑫ Bear right downhill to cross the stile and descend steps to a white track, once the main road into **Compton village**. Turn left to follow the track between thick hedgerows twined with wild clematis and bryony. This leads past a quarry and uphill to the National Trust car park on **Spreadeagle Hill**. To return to the **Compton Abbas airfield**, turn right, with the road on your left, to the stile onto **Clubmen's Down** – point 2 – and, retracing your steps, turn left along the lane to the car park entrance.

Date walk completed:

Walk 15

BERE REGIS AND THE VALLEY OF THE RIVER PUDDLE

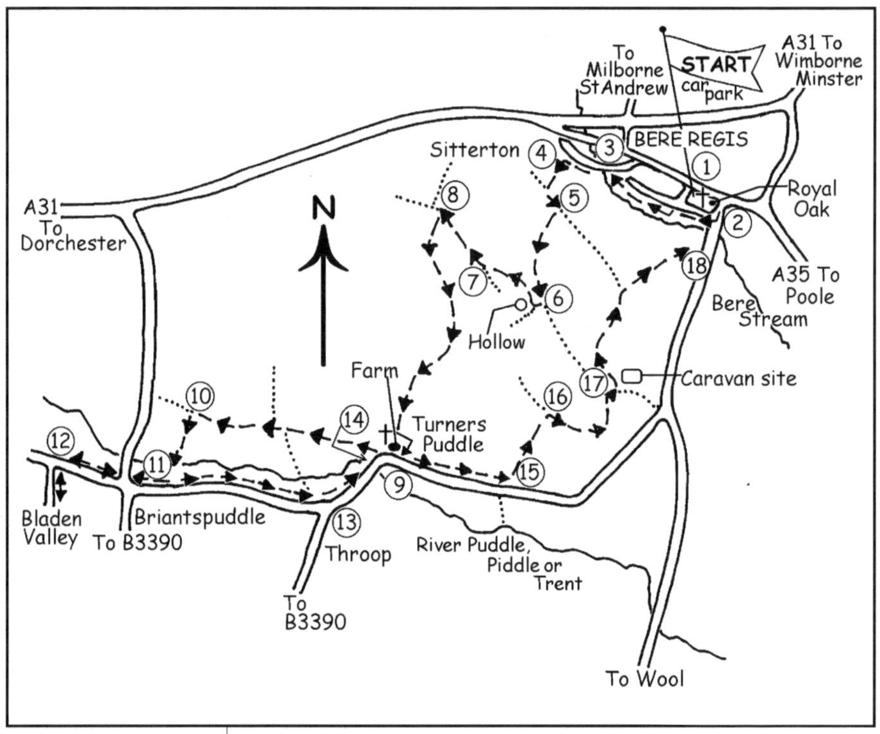

Distance:
7 miles

Starting point:
The car park near the church.
GR 847948

Map: OS Explorer 117 Cerne Abbas and Bere Regis

How to get there: *Bere Regis is about 12 miles east of Dorchester. Turn for Bere Regis off the A35 (the Poole-Dorchester road), which meets the A31 just north of the village. Follow the road sign for Wool, passing the Royal Oak on your right. After about 50yds turn right, following the car park sign. Another right turn shortly afterwards takes you to the car park on your right.*

THE BOARDWALK BESIDE THE BERE STREAM

Once great areas of heathland stretched across the heart of Dorset, immortalised by Thomas Hardy as 'Egdon'. Although much of this once wild country is now pine forest, south of Bere Regis you can still walk on the splendid open heath that Hardy knew. The route of this walk crosses part of this windswept upland but we begin with a ramble from Bere Regis beside the Bere Stream to Sitterton (or Shitterton, whichever you prefer), a charming village of thatched colour-washed houses. From the village sunken tracks lead up to the heath. Glorious views unfold as we cross this high country and descend into one of Dorset's loveliest valleys, threaded by the River Puddle. (The river is also known as the Piddle or the Trent.) From the old world village of Briantspuddle we make a short detour to Bladen Valley, a model village built for his workers by Sir Ernest Debenham between 1919 and 1932. The route climbs through my favourite bluebell wood before crossing the heath again and returning to Bere Regis.

The Royal Oak in Bere Regis is an old coaching inn dating from early in the 17th century. Before the construction of the bypass many weary travellers must have enjoyed a warm welcome at this friendly inn as it faces the once busy meeting of the roads from Dorchester, Wimborne, Poole and Wool. Now the scene may be more peaceful but the welcome is just as warm. The bar area is spacious and there is a comfortable, separate dining room. Real ales include Flowers Original, Ringwood and Abbot. Draught cider and a selection of wines are also on offer. Popular dishes include rib-eye steak and delicious old-fashioned faggots, peas and mash. Also on the menu when we called were whole local trout and home-made lasagne. For a sweet you could sample chocolate fudge gateau, meringue nest or treacle sponge. There is a secluded beer garden. For a longer stay the **Royal Oak** offers accommodation.

The pub is open *every day from 11 am to 11 pm and food is served from 12 noon to 2 pm and in the evening from 7 pm to 9 pm.*
Telephone: 01929 471203.

① Follow the direction of the sign for **Bere Regis church** from the car park. Readers of Thomas Hardy will recognise the church as the setting for some of the scenes in his novel *Tess of the d'Urbervilles*. Hardy slightly altered the name of a real family, the Turbervilles, who were lords of the manor of Bere Regis for 500 years from the 13th to the 18th century.

Just before you come to the south porch you will see the Turberville tombs with the family vault beneath on your right. On the grass above, the homeless Durbeyfield family set up their four poster bed overlooked by the beautiful square-arched Tudor window bearing the Turberville crest and coat of arms. Tess recalls that her family have a seal and a spoon bearing these insignia.

Inside the church there is much of interest but its glory is the magnificent 15th-century roof of the nave. It is constructed entirely of oak with brightly painted, almost life-size figures of the twelve apostles dressed as Tudor gentlemen leaning at right angles from the supports, as if keeping an eye on the congregation. It was the gift of a native of the area, Cardinal John Morton, Archbishop of Canterbury and Chancellor to Henry VII.

② From the church walk down to the **Wool** road. Turn right down the road and after a few yards turn right again to follow **Elder Road** until you come to **Manor Farm Road** on your right. Turn left to walk over the grass to the boardwalk beside the **Bere Stream**. Bear right along the boardwalk with the stream on your left. This raised footway is a delight. Shaded by willows, it carries you dry-shod over marshes spiked with yellow irises. As you come to drier ground the boardwalk gives way to a path. Bear slightly left to continue heading west past a bridge on the left. A gravel path brings you to a lane in **Sitterton**.

③ Turn left over a bridge to enjoy a walk through the village. Keep to the lane as it curves right. Ignore the first footpath on the left (it is marked with the **Jubilee Trail** sign – a white arrow on a green background – which we follow later). Continue through the village then, opposite number 7, turn left up the next footpath, also marked with the **Jubilee Trail** sign.

④ Follow the path uphill to a crossing track. Turn left and keep ahead for about 150yds.

⑤ At this point you come to a junction. Be careful here! Turn right, uphill, towards the heath, beneath

THE 17TH-CENTURY COACHING INN, BERE REGIS

pollarded hazels to reach a small iron gate.

⑥ Go through the gate and, following the **Jubilee Trail** sign, turn right. After a few yards the path divides in front of a hollow. Take the right hand path (the route differs from the OS map until point 7). A narrow path now dips and winds over the heath and finally rises to meet a wide green crosstrack.

⑦ Turn right to follow this ridge path with fine views over the valley of the **Bere Stream** on your right and the **Puddle valley** on your left. Keep ahead through a gate until you come to a small iron gate.

⑧ Through the gate turn immediately left (ignore bridleway signs a short distance ahead) and follow the **Jubilee Trail** down a pleasant path leading down into the **Puddle valley**. In front of the gate into the farm turn left. Go through a small wooden gate to a crosspath and turn right. The path leads through gates to the lane in **Turners Puddle**.

⑨ Turn right to pass the tiny church which stands on a grassy terrace overlooking the river.

Some of the names on the gravestones – Talbut and Chamberlayne – are reminders that King John built a palace and held court at Bere Regis in 1205. The grassed-over foundations can be seen in the field opposite the turning to the church beside the Wool road.

When the lane swings left for **Throop** keep straight on along the gravel track through the valley with the river running through the meadows on your left. Follow the track for almost a mile past the footpaths to **Throop** and **Kite Hill**.

⑩ Turn left, following the sign for **Briantspuddle**. Cross a meadow and the bridge over the river, then bear slightly left over the next meadow towards the houses of the village. Go over a stile and join the road through the village. We make a short detour here to see this attractive village and visit **Bladen Valley**.

⑪ Turn right through the village. Cross a road and keep ahead, following the sign for **Affpuddle** and **Bladen Valley**. After about 1/4 mile **Bladen Valley** is on your left, a beautifully laid-out estate with houses overlooking wide greens set with flowering trees. The tall, slender war memorial at the entrance to the village is by Eric Gill.

⑫ Turn right to retrace your steps through **Briantspuddle** and follow the road in the direction of **Throop**. Opposite **Cruck Cottage** is the model dairy, an attractive building resembling a row of almshouses, built by Sir Ernest Debenham. Cross the wide-paved approach to the dairy and continue for about $^1/_2$ mile to Throop.

⑬ When the road turns sharply right through the village keep straight on along a gravel track marked by a sign with a white T. Leave the gravel when it curves right and follow the pleasant narrow lane ahead, heading east along the valley with the **Puddle** on your left. The river swings south across our way. Cross the footbridge and follow the track as it bears left and cross another footbridge to the lane in **Turners Puddle**.

⑭ Turn right to pass the farm, now on your left, and follow the lane for a little over $^1/_2$ mile. Pass a bridleway sign on your right.

⑮ A few yards further on look very carefully for a footpath sign on your left indicating a narrow path leading left uphill into a wood. Turn left to follow this path as it climbs gently through the trees, bordered by a sea of bluebells in May. You leave the wood to emerge on the open hillside with the heath rising ahead. Keep straight on uphill to a narrow crosspath.

⑯ Turn right along a path which dips a little then runs along the hillside before bearing left uphill to a stile by a gate. Cross the stile to a gravel track. Turn right and go downhill for about 30yds to a gate on your left by a bridleway sign.

⑰ Turn left through the gate and follow the path with fencing at first on your right. You pass a caravan site on your right. The path leads through the trees to an iron gate. Go through the gate and follow the track downhill towards **Bere Regis**. As you approach the houses you reach a lane which curves right and left twice to bring you to the **Wool** road.

⑱ Turn left to cross the **Bere Stream** then left again along **Elder Road** to return to the car park.

Walk 16

STUDLAND – A WALK IN THE PURBECK HILLS

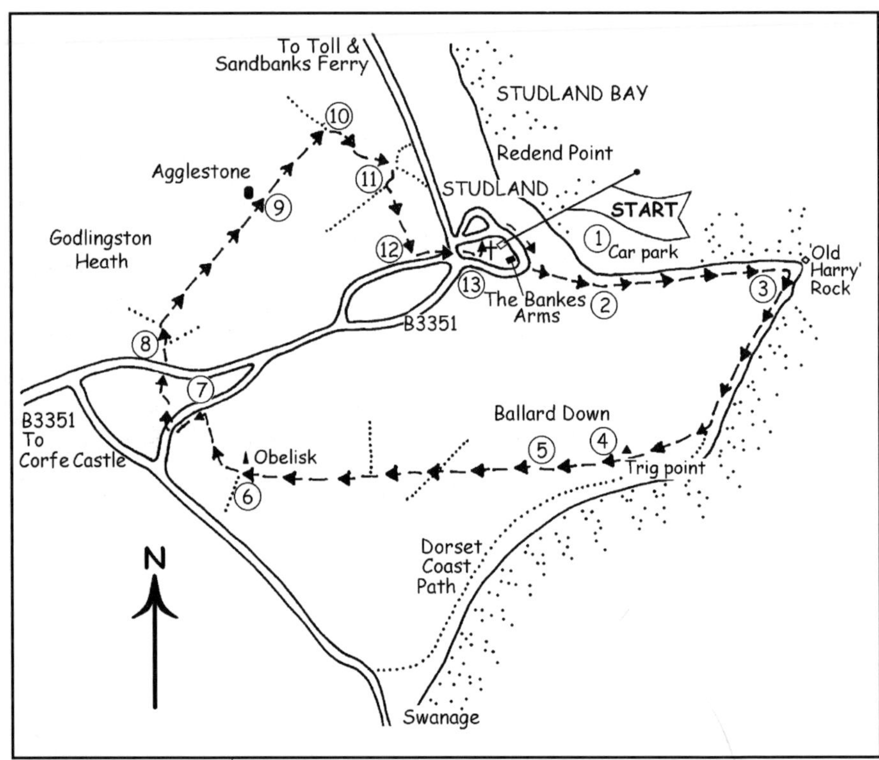

Distance:
$7^1/_2$ miles

Starting point:
The National Trust car park on the right beside the Bankes Arms. The car park is open from 9 am to 11 pm. GR 038825

Map: OS Outdoor Leisure 15 Purbeck and South Dorset

How to get there: *Head south along the A351 towards Corfe Castle village. Turn left under the railway bridge along the B3351, signed 'Studland 5 miles'. Drive into the village, turn right, following the sign for the Manor Hotel, then right, and right again, following the large brown signs for the Bankes Arms.*

THE AGGLESTONE POISED PRECARIOUSLY ON GODLINGSTON HEATH

The Isle of Purbeck is famous for its spectacular scenery and wealth of wildlife. This walk reveals some of the finest aspects of this splendid part of Dorset. We start in Studland, an attractive village beside a small bay of gently shelving sand, hidden from the sea by copse woods and orchards. From the village we follow a clifftop path to the Foreland, the eastern tip of the great chalk ridge which stretches across the Isle of Purbeck from Lulworth Cove in the west, ending in a series of sheer-sided pinnacles and arches including the famous 'Old Harry' stack. Our path then leads along the crest of Ballard Down with magnificent views seawards over Swanage Bay and inland over Godlingston Heath and Poole Harbour. We descend the down to cross the heath to the Agglestone, a huge sandstone rock with a menacing overhang poised precariously on a mound. Woodland paths lead back to Studland past the splendid Norman church.

Until 1981, when Ralph Bankes gave the Purbecks to the National Trust, the area was part of the Kingston Lacy and Corfe Castle Estate owned by his family. The very popular pub where we begin this walk bears their name. The **Bankes Arms** is a genuine, friendly village pub with a garden overlooking the sea. There is a choice of eight real ales plus a guest beer so there should be sufficient to suit all tastes! A wide range of excellent food is on offer with locally caught fish a speciality. The menu includes a variety of salads and ploughman's, and interesting dishes such as whole, shell-on king prawns in garlic butter and hot, smoked mackerel fillets with horseradish sauce. Delicious home-made chicken-and-mushroom or steak-and-kidney pies and steaks cooked to your liking will satisfy the heartiest of appetites. Dogs are welcome. Overnight accommodation is available.

In summer the pub is open *from 11 am to 11 pm, in winter from 11 am to 3 pm and from 7 pm to 11.30 pm. Meals are served from 12 noon to 9.30 pm from June to the end of October. At other times check beforehand by telephone. Telephone: 01929 450225.*

① Turn right from the car park entrance to pass the **Bankes Arms** on your right. Walk down the hill and at the foot turn left and follow the sign '**Footpath to Old Harry**'. The path goes through a gate then tunnels through trees and bushes with glimpses of **Studland beach** on your left.

A more peaceful scene would be hard to imagine but during the Second World War a rehearsal for the D-Day landings in Normandy took place here. In the exercise, code-named 'Exercise Smash', Studland was 'attacked' with live ammunition. Troops and tanks stormed ashore watched by the Allied commanders from a bunker, Fort Henry, on Redend Point not far from the Bankes Arms.

② You emerge on open downland with fine views over the approach to **Poole Harbour** on the left and the **Isle of Wight** ahead. The springy turf is rich in wild flowers, attracting hordes of butterflies including the migrant Painted Lady and the Clouded Yellow. The path leads east to **the Foreland** to reveal dramatic scenery. Gleaming white cliffs rise vertically from the sea as if sliced by a knife and, separated from the mainland by a narrow gulf, the arch of '**Old Harry**' still defies the force of the waves. It was possibly christened '**Old Harry**', a name for the Devil, by sailors who knew its dangers when, in Thomas Hardy's words, it appeared 'like a skeleton's lower jaw, grinning at British navigation'.

③ Bear right and follow the wider path indicated a little later by posts (the **Dorset Coast Path**) along the headland towards **Ballard Point**. Keep to the **Coast Path**, with a fence on your right, past a bridleway on the right. When you come to a marker stone continue along the **Coast Path**, passing the stone on your left. Go through a gate and leave the **Coast Path**, which descends the hillside on the left for **Swanage**, and take the path which bears slightly right past a trig point.

④ Continue across a dip and now a wide path leads ahead, rising gently along the crest of **Ballard Down**. Apart from the panoramic views there is much more to enjoy as you follow this upland path. Larks sing overhead and in spring and summer the close-grazed turf is starred with wild flowers. Low-growing red and yellow flowered vetches, marjoram and carline thistles attract butterflies such as the rare Adonis Blue and the distinctive Marbled White.

⑤ Go through a gate and keep ahead signed '**To the Obelisk**'. Continue for almost a mile, passing two footpaths on the right. The path rises to lead through a gate and between fences. A short descent brings you to the pencil-shaped **Obelisk**.

It stands on a plinth of Purbeck marble and is composed of five sections of white Devonshire granite. It began life as a lamp standard outside the church of St Mary Woolnoth in the City of London. George Burt, the powerful Victorian speculator, brought it to Swanage and had it erected on Ballard Down in 1892 to mark the opening of nearby Ulwell reservoir. Demolished in 1941 it was re-erected in 1973 by the 129 East Riding Field Squadron Royal Engineers (Volunteers).

⑥ Pass the **Obelisk** on your right, go through a gate and follow the path ahead as it drops downhill and bears right through a gate. Continue down the grassy path and go through a gate to a minor road.

⑦ Turn left along the wide verge. As the road begins to curve left turn right, following the direction of the footpath sign over a stile. Navigate carefully here! Turn half-right and walk up the side of the hill to cross another stile leading to a narrow path through a wood. The path broadens as it winds uphill through the trees to a golf course. Keep ahead for about 100yds to a post with a yellow arrow footpath sign. Turn right as the sign directs to cross a stile to the B3351.

⑧ Turn left for just a few yards to the entrance to **Godlingston Heath Nature Reserve** on your right. Turn right through two small wooden gates and follow the narrow path downhill between bushes at first. Then follow the heathland paths over the reserve, signed for the **Agglestone**.

The reserve is nationally important for its rich wildlife. Rare sand lizards breed here and birds include hobbies and nightjars, the latter sounding like crickets. You may spot the small Sika deer, instantly recognisable by his flared white rump when alarmed.

The path leads through double gates and over a crosstrack then dips to reveal your first sight of the **Agglestone**.

No one seems to know how this huge lump of rock arrived here. According to legend the Devil was passing some time on the Isle of Wight when he decided to hurl the rock at Corfe Castle. He missed his aim and it landed on Godlingston Heath instead. 'Agglestone' could be derived from Anglo-Saxon 'Haligstan',

THE BANKES ARMS, STUDLAND

meaning 'The Holy Stone' giving quite a different slant to the legend!

⑨ Leave the **Agglestone** on your left and follow the narrow path steeply downhill then across a valley to a crosspath.

⑩ Bear right and follow a broad woodland path for about 100yds. Turn right over a footbridge then bear slightly right again through a gate. Follow the track ahead, which curves left and sinks deep between banks of ferns and becomes gravelled as it leads past some houses. Look carefully for a footpath on the right. (Bridleways are marked on a gatepost on the left.)

⑪ Turn right through the trees for about 150 yards then bear left at a Y-junction. Take the narrow path to the left of a wire fence, then follow the track ahead to a minor road.

⑫ Turn left, cross the main B3351 and keep ahead down **School Lane**.

⑬ After about 150yds turn left up a footpath signed '**To the Church**' and walk through the graveyard to the church.

This magnificent church overlooking the sea is dedicated appropriately to St Nicholas, patron saint of sailors and fishermen. The earliest building dates from the first years of the 11th century but it was remodelled in the 12th century by Norman craftsmen and remains a splendid example of their work, with rounded arches and finely groined and vaulted roofs. The tower was left unfinished. Perhaps the builders feared the foundations would not support the weight of the extra masonry involved.

Opposite the south porch is the grave of Sergeant Lawrence of the 40th Regiment of Foot. He fought in all the battles of the Peninsular War and finally at Waterloo. During the occupation of Paris he met and married a French girl and when peace returned he brought her home to Studland to help him run the village pub.

Leave with the side of the church on your right and take the narrow path that runs alongside the car park to the road. Turn right to return to your car.

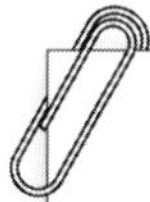

Date walk completed:

Walk 17

STURMINSTER MARSHALL, BADBURY RINGS AND SHAPWICK

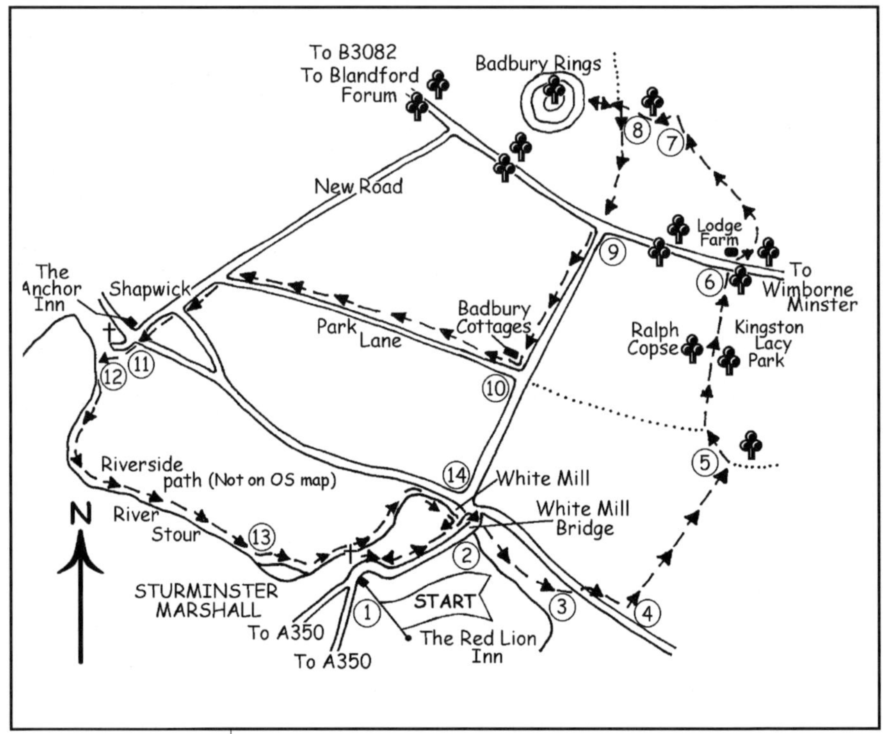

Distance:
9 miles

Starting point:
The Red Lion Inn car park. GR 951004

Map: OS Explorer 118 Shaftesbury and Cranborne Chase

How to get there: *Sturminster Marshall lies east of the A350 between Blandford Forum and Poole. Turn off the A350 following the sign for the village centre. Drive through the village and the Red Lion is on your right opposite the church.*

MEDIEVAL WHITE MILL BRIDGE CROSSED AT THE START OF THE WALK

A few miles north-west of Wimborne Minster the river Stour runs through a wide valley bordered by lush meadows. This lovely countryside, part of the extensive Kingston Lacy Estate now owned by the National Trust, forms the setting for this walk. Apart from a rich variety of wildlife you will discover a great deal more to enjoy as you follow field paths and country lanes and take a leisurely ramble by the riverside. The route includes two attractive villages, Sturminster Marshall and Shapwick, White Mill, with a history dating back to the Domesday Book, medieval White Mill Bridge, one of Dorset's oldest bridges, and Badbury Rings, a splendid Iron Age hill fort built by a Celtic tribe, the Durotriges. Their Roman conquerors made Badbury the meeting place for two roads: the Ackling Dyke, connecting Salisbury and Dorchester, and an important road connecting their spa town, Bath, with Poole Harbour.

Our starting point is the **Red Lion Inn** in Sturminster Marshall. This traditional village inn dates from the early 18th century and once stood beside an old road leading east from Dorchester to Wimborne. Now it stands in a peaceful corner of the village overlooking the meadows beside the Stour. The bar area is cosy and attractive with blazing log fires in cold weather and there is an excellent non-smoking restaurant. All the food is made to order and is well worth waiting for. Many dishes feature local game, along with fresh fish and seafood. You are sure to find a meal to suit as the range is wide and varied, from fish and chips and bar snacks to exotic dishes like kangaroo. From the specials board we selected a crab and red pepper salsa tortilla and honey roasted ham hock with a raspberry sauce. Real ales are Badger Best and Tanglefoot and guest ales. The wine list is extensive and well chosen.

Opening times *are from 12 noon to 2.30 pm and from 7 pm to 11 pm; Sundays from 12 noon to 3 pm and from 7 pm to 10.30 pm. Food is served from 12 noon to 2 pm and from 7 pm to 9.30 pm (9 pm on Sundays.) Children under fourteen are not allowed in the restaurant in the evening.*
Telephone: 01258 857319.

① Leave with the front of the pub on your right and the church on your left and follow **Church Lane** past an attractive row of thatched cottages restored in memory of Thomas Hardy by the Society for the Protection of Ancient Buildings. The lane runs between the meadows to a beautiful stretch of the **Stour** crossed by **White Mill Bridge**.

There has been a bridge on this site since 1174. It is built in Norman style with eight arches resting on 800-year-old oak piles. The arches are attractively ribbed with alternate layers of white limestone and red sandstone. As on several bridges in Dorset a plaque warns that anyone caught damaging the structure will be transported!

White Mill, on the opposite bank of the river, was substantially rebuilt in 1776 but there was probably a mill on this site as early as the 11th century. Now restored by the National Trust, the mill is open for guided tours at weekends between Easter and October from 12 noon to 5 pm.

② Cross the bridge to a signpost on the right. Leave the lane and turn right over the stile (all the stiles on this walk are the V-shaped, squeeze variety), following the sign for the **Stour Valley Way**. The path runs through fields with the river on your right then narrows between hedges before crossing another stile and more open meadows. Keep to the path as it bears a little left away from the river over a final stile.

③ Navigate carefully here! About 30yds after the stile turn left up the bank, go over a stile and cross the field ahead. Over the next stile you reach a lane. Turn right along the lane for about 200yds.

④ Turn left, following the direction of the bridleway sign through a gate and follow the wide grassy track ahead for about $^3/_4$ mile to a crosspath in front of the belt of woodland protecting **Kingston Lacy Park**.

⑤ Turn left to follow **Kingston Lacy Drove** with the woods on your right. The **Drove** bears right past a joining track on the left and leads between wooded parkland and **Ralph Copse**, a sea of bluebells in May. The **Drove** leads for about a mile to a gate. Go through the gate and across a parking area to the main **Blandford Road**, B3082. The

THE RED LION, STURMINSTER MARSHALL

road is bordered by the famous avenue of pollarded beech trees planted by William John Bankes in 1835 as an anniversary gift for his mother.

⑥ Cross the road and bear right over the grass for a few yards. Go past a wooden barrier to the asphalt drive signed for **Lodge Farm**. Turn left along the drive then take the footpath ahead to a small iron gate. We continue through the gate but look left here to see **Lodge Farm**. It is a fascinating building – either a late medieval house or an ancient barn converted into a dwelling in the 1600s. The upper floor has two 15th-century windows with traceried heads. Follow the footpath beside meadows with a hedge on your left. The path curves left and climbs gently towards a wood.

⑦ Turn left in front of the wood and follow the path as it bears left to reveal a splendid view of the triple embankments of **Badbury Rings** hill fort and brings you to a crosstrack.

⑧ Bear right for a few yards to a stile on your left. To explore **the Rings**, cross the stile and walk over the grass ahead to the eastern entrance. Although the summit is only 330ft above sea level you enjoy a magnificent view of the **Needles** and the **Isle of Wight**, the **Purbeck peninsula** and the **vale of the Stour**.

It is possible that this impressive fort was the Mount Badon of the Saxon chronicles where, in AD 520, the legendary Arthur, leading an army of Romanised Celts, defeated an invading Saxon army under Cedric. As a result the West of England was saved from conquest for 50 years. But there are other possible sites for the battle, including Bath and Badbury hill fort near Swindon.

Retrace your steps and go over the stile to return to the crosstrack at point 8. Turn right (left if you did not cross the stile to **the Rings**) and walk downhill, with a hedge on your right, to the B3082.

⑨ Cross straight over and follow the lane ahead signed for **Sturminster Marshall**. The lane rises to **Badbury Cottages**.

⑩ Just past the cottages turn right along **Park Lane**, signed for **Shapwick**. Follow this pleasant, quiet lane for about $1\frac{1}{4}$ miles to the junction with **New Road** and turn left to walk through **Shapwick village**. The course of the Roman road runs parallel just over the hedge on the left. **Shapwick** is a tranquil village with many thatched houses built of brick or cob. The village cross stands in the centre of a small square. It retains its original Saxon steps.

Opposite the cross you will find the Anchor Inn – just the spot for a little light refreshment before tackling the end of the walk! Excellent home-cooked food is available, every day except Monday, between 12 noon and 2 pm and 7 pm and 9 pm. Opening times are from 11.30 am to 3 pm and 6.30 pm to 11 pm on Monday to Saturday, 12 noon to 3.30 pm and 7 pm to 10.30 pm on Sunday. Real ales are Ringwood Best Bitter, Abbot Ale and York Brewery's Swing Low. Telephone: 01258 857269.

⑪ Leave the cross on your right and continue along the lane ahead, signed '**Stour Valley Way White Mill**'. Follow the lane as it curves right for a few yards then turn left to cross the church car park. Go over a stile and keep ahead over the grass towards the **Stour**, passing the church and churchyard on your right.

⑫ Bear left to follow the riverside path over a wooden footbridge to walk through the meadows, crossing several stiles. Beside you the river flows shaded by willows and bordered by tall stands of reeds and yellow irises. Follow the river for about 1¼ miles.

⑬ At this point, after crossing a stile, the path turns left for a few yards then right to resume its easterly heading with a fence on your right. Continue beside fields and over stiles with a small stream on your right to rejoin the riverside. The path follows the river as it curves left past the houses of **Sturminster Marshall** on the opposite bank. Past the village keep following the river as it curves right. The path finally leaves the river and leads up steps to a lane.

⑭ Turn right along the lane past **White Mill** and turn right again over **White Mill Bridge** to retrace your steps to **Sturminster Marshall** and the **Red Lion Inn**.

Date walk completed:

FARNHAM AND THE VALLEY OF THE TARRANT

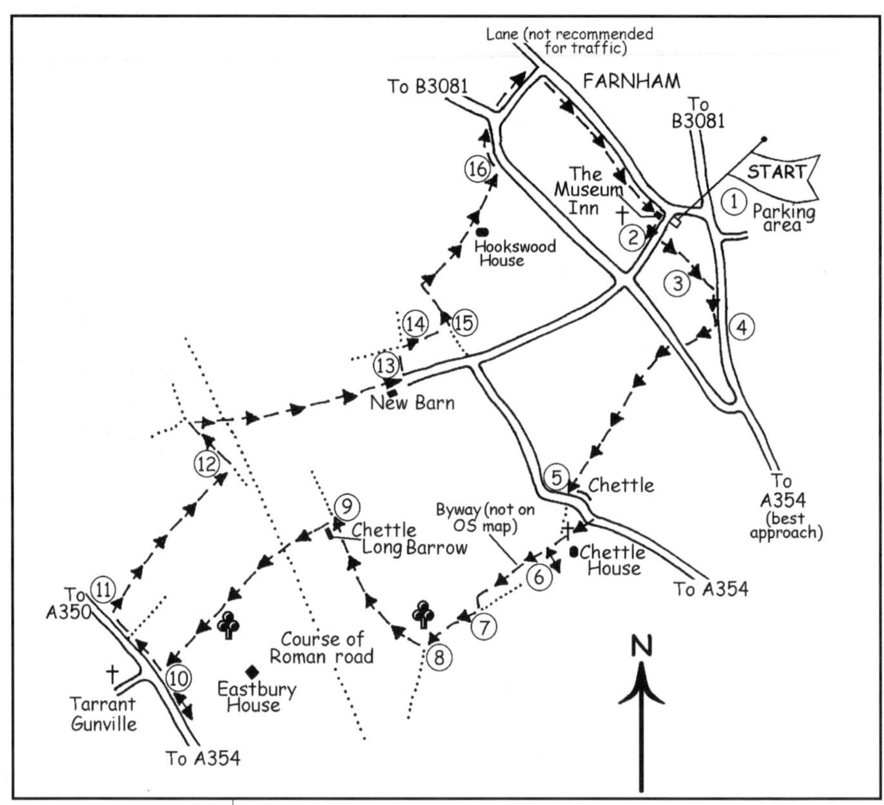

Distance:
$8^1/_2$ miles

Starting point:
The parking area in front of the children's playground. GR 959151

Map: OS Explorer 118 Shaftesbury and Cranborne Chase

How to get there: *Farnham is best approached from the south via the A354 Blandford-Salisbury road. Turn for Farnham, following the sign at Thickthorn Cross. Take the first turning on the left. The road curves right to a T-junction. Turn right to drive downhill into the village. The Museum Inn is on your left just before a T-junction in the village. The parking area is opposite, on your right, in front of the children's playground.*

CHETTLE HOUSE IS AN EARLY 18TH-CENTURY MANSION

This is a splendid walk in the heart of Cranborne Chase, close to the Wiltshire border. We start from Farnham, one of Dorset's prettiest villages. As in most downland villages the houses face each other across a narrow street with a stream playing hide and seek on either side. Most of the houses are dark thatched with colour-washed or flint walls attractively banded with brick. The church of St Lawrence, which has a 12th-century nave, is hidden away beyond the large, tree-shaded village green. We follow upland paths before heading downhill into a remote valley to discover Chettle, a tiny cluster of farms and cottages in a wooded hollow, overlooked by a manor house. Paths through coppiced woodland rich in wild flowers lead to the parkland and fine trees surrounding Eastbury House and Tarrant Gunville, the most northerly of the Tarrant villages, close to the source of the stream. The return route crosses the line of a Roman road and the site of a Celtic settlement before a quiet grass-bordered lane leads us back to Farnham.

The **Museum Inn** is an attractive and friendly hostelry dating back to the 17th century. Originally it was called the Yew Tree (there are still two close to the building, sheltering the village stocks). The inn owes its present name to the archaeologist General Augustus Lane Fox Pitt Rivers, who inherited the huge Rushmore Estate, which included Farnham, at the end of the 19th century. He housed the results of his excavations in a former school for gypsies in the village. This is now a private house but some of his collection can be seen in Salisbury Museum. The General also established the nearby Larmer Tree Gardens, which then, as now, attracted many visitors. The inn offered them accommodation and refreshments meeting the General's high standards. 'It is exceedingly clean and well managed,' he wrote, 'and the food good.' I think, after your visit, you will agree with the General!

Whenever possible the chef uses local suppliers. Poultry is free-range and game comes from neighbouring estates. Favourite starters include chicken liver parfait with plum chutney and fettucine pasta with smoked bacon and wild mushrooms. For a main course confit of duck with lentils de Puy and coriander and, from the fish menu, fillets of John Dory are popular. When we called, real ales were Ringwood Best, Exmoor Gold and Tanglefoot. For a longer stay excellent accommodation is available.

The inn is open *Monday to Saturday from 12 noon to 3 pm and from 6 pm to 11 pm; Sunday from 12 noon to 3 pm and from 7 pm to 10 pm. Meals are served from 12 noon to 2 pm and from 7 pm to 9.30 pm; Sunday from 12 noon to 3 pm and from 7 pm to 9 pm.*
Telephone: 01725 516261.

① Leaving the phone box and children's playground on your left walk up the lane signed for **Chettle**. As you pass the lane to the church look over the grass on your right to see the 100-year-old roofed **Well House**. Continue uphill for about 50yds.

② Turn left, following the direction of the footpath sign, and cross the stile. Keep ahead beside three fields, crossing more stiles.

③ At this point you are faced by an open field. Walk straight over the field towards a small electrical installation. Cross the stile in front of the installation and turn right up a lane.

④ After about 100yds turn right, in

the direction of a bridleway sign and the green sign for the Ramblers' **Jubilee Trail**. The path runs beside fields with a hedge on your right. Go through a gate to a lane. Bear right for a few yards then turn left to continue along the bridleway, still following the **Jubilee Trail**. Go through a gate and keep ahead beside a field with a hedge on the left. The path leads through two more gates and beside another field, still with a hedge on your left. Then it dips gently downhill through a wooden gate before rising a little to run between hedges. Now an attractive green track leads down into the **Chettle valley** to meet a crossing lane in **Chettle village**.

⑤ Turn left along the lane (temporarily leaving the **Jubilee Trail**, which takes a footpath on the right). Pass **Chettle stores** and about 100yds further on turn right, signed for **Chettle House**, and walk uphill, passing the church on the left (where we rejoin the **Jubilee Trail**) and the drive to **Chettle House**.

⑥ Our way is straight ahead along the byway through the park. But before following it turn left to walk a few yards through the trees to enjoy a fine view of the west front of **Chettle House** and the gardens.

Chettle House is an early 18th-century mansion designed by

THE 17TH-CENTURY MUSEUM INN AT FARNHAM

Thomas Archer and built by the Bastard family for George Chafin, MP. After falling into disrepair it was bought in 1840 and restored by Edward Castleman, the promoter of the first railway through Dorset. The curved ends were added in 1912 to match the existing rounded entrance front.

Chettle House is open Easter to early October, every day except Tuesday and Saturday, 11 am to 5 pm. Plants for sale. Telephone: 01258 830209.

Retrace your steps and follow the byway through the park. (The present right of way differs slightly from the OS map.) This is a lovely walk shaded by magnificent oak and beech trees. The byway curves left then right to meet a crosstrack.

⑦ Turn right uphill to go through a gate. The trees of **Little Wood** are on your right. Keep straight ahead (left hand path) through woods of coppiced hazels.

⑧ Before an iron gate bear right to continue through the coppice woods. The trees give way to an open field. Continue beside the field with a strip of woodland on your left. After about 1/4 mile you pass the raised embankment of **Chettle Long Barrow** on your left. Here the first farmers on these downs buried their dead over 4,000 years ago.

⑨ Just after the barrow look carefully for a stile on your left marked with the **Jubilee Trail** sign. Turn left over the stile. Bear left, with a hedge on your left, then bear right to walk beside a field. Cross a stile and a farm track and continue along a wide grassy hedged track. A splendid view over the **Tarrant valley** opens ahead. The track curves left for a few yards then right to enter the parkland surrounding **Eastbury House**. Walk through the park with a hedge on your right and a fine avenue of trees a few yards away on your left. Past the avenue you can catch a glimpse of **Eastbury House**.

Only one wing remains of this once magnificent mansion designed by Vanbrugh to rival Blenheim Palace and built in the early 18th century for the dandy George Bubb Doddington. It was too large and expensive to maintain and after his death and that of his nephew most of the house was demolished. The house and one of the gateways can be seen from the road through Tarrant Gunville.

Bear a little left to go through a small iron gate and walk through a wood. A narrow path leads to a lane which brings you to the road in **Tarrant Gunville**.

⑩ Our way is right here but to see

Eastbury House turn left for about 100yds. Then retrace your steps through this attractive village with the **Tarrant** running under tiny bridges on your right, passing a footpath on the right.

⑪ After just over 1/4 mile turn right up a hedged asphalt lane which soon becomes a grassy track. Cross a stile and continue uphill, passing a small wood on your right. Go over the next stile to a farm track.

⑫ Turn left to a crosstrack then leave the farm track and turn right. After about 200yds you cross the line of a Roman road heading north from **Badbury Rings**. Continue past a gate and through a copse for about a mile to **New Barn** on your right.

⑬ Just past the barn turn left through a gate. The path runs downhill then curves a little left over a field towards woodland. The embankments in front of the woods are part of the remains of a Celtic village.

⑭ Ignore a track directly ahead (not a right of way) and turn right, following the bridleway arrow. Continue beside a field, hedge on right, for about 1/4 mile to a crosstrack.

⑮ Turn left up the field to meet a hedge. Turn right with the hedge on your left. The path curves slightly left through bushes then runs downhill past **Hookswood House** on your right. Follow the white track straight ahead to meet a road at **New Town**.

⑯ Bear left up the road for about 200yds to a junction – watch for traffic. At the junction turn right to follow a pleasant lane running downhill and curving right to lead you through **Farnham** village to your car.

Date walk completed:

Walk 19

GUSSAGE ALL SAINTS AND ACKLING DYKE

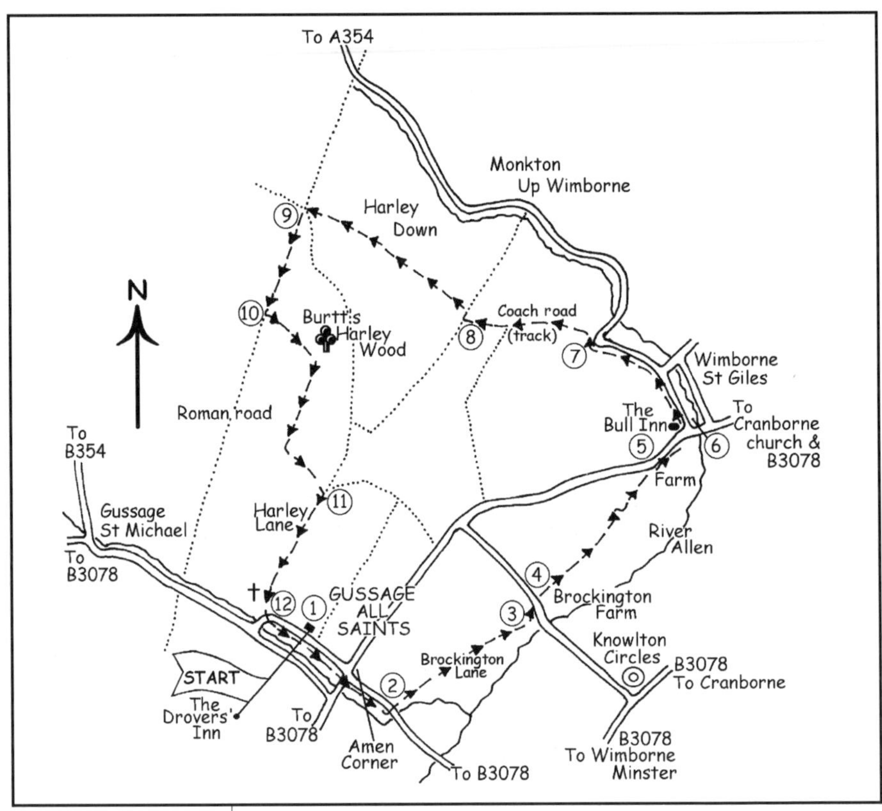

Distance:
$8\frac{1}{2}$ miles

Starting point:
The Drovers' Inn car park. Have a word with the management before you leave your car to start the walk. GR 003107

Map: OS Explorer 118 Shaftesbury and Cranborne Chase

How to get there: *Gussage All Saints is about 7 miles east of Blandford Forum. Best approached via the A354 Blandford Forum-Salisbury road. Turn for the village at Cashmoor, drive through Gussage St Michael and bear left over the Gussage stream. The main road through the village curves right and the Drovers' Inn is on your left.*

The rolling uplands of Cranborne Chase are wonderful walking country, sheltering in their valleys many attractive villages. This walk links two of the most delightful, Gussage All Saints and Wimborne St Giles. They are very different in their appeal. Gussage All Saints lies, serene and peaceful, tucked away in a remote valley threaded by a clear chalk stream. Wimborne St Giles is a spacious village set in lush, wooded countryside at the centre of the Shaftesbury Estate. From earliest times man has settled these hills. Although much of the downland is now farmed the tracks followed by the drovers and their flocks remain. From Gussage All Saints we take these grassy ways high on the downs giving wide views over the Chase. Our return route follows part of Ackling Dyke, a road constructed by the Romans in the first century AD to link two important towns, Old Sarum, just north of Salisbury, and Durnovaria, today's Dorchester.

If you enjoy traditional country fare in a genuine old world pub then look no further than the **Drovers' Inn** in Gussage All Saints. You will receive a warm welcome in this comfortable hostelry with its heavily-beamed ceilings, flagged floors, tiny deep-set windows and enormous fireplaces. Here you can sample home cooking at its best. We found locally produced pork pies with hand raised crusts and venison sausages among the dishes on the menu and some delicious old-fashioned sweets which included Grandma's sticky toffee pudding! Ploughman's lunches came with a dazzling selection of cheeses. Real ales on offer are Ringwood Best, Fortyniner, True Glory and Old Thumper. Cider is on tap and there is a good selection of wines. In fine weather you can sit in the pleasant garden overlooking the valley.

Opening times *are from 11 am to 3 pm and 6 pm to 11 pm; Sundays from 12 noon to 2.30 pm and 7 pm to 10.30 pm. Food is served from 12 noon to 2 pm and 7 pm to 9 pm.*
Telephone: 01258 840084.

ON ACKLING DYKE – THE EMBANKMENT PROBABLY INDICATES THE ROAD'S ORIGINAL HEIGHT

The Walk

① Starting with the front of the pub on your left follow the road through the village. When you come to the crossroads at the intriguingly named '**Amen Corner**' cross straight over and continue along the lane signed for **Bowerswain**. The lane rises a little then drops downhill into a valley.

② Just before you come to a small bridge over a stream turn left to follow a footpath – marked on the map as **Brockington Lane** – with the stream on your right. After about 80yds our grassy path bears slightly left to leave the stream and run between hedges. Soon the path narrows and becomes more wooded, bordered in spring with violets and bluebells. Keep ahead for almost a mile to meet a wider track.
Turn left (ignore a stile leading

into a field directly ahead) and walk to a lane in front of **Brockington Farm**.

③ Turn left along the lane, passing farm buildings on your right. Follow the lane as it curves right as far as a sharp left bend.

④ Leave the lane here and bear right, following the direction of the footpath sign along a gravel track. An old wall draped in ivy is on your right. Look through the large gaps in the wall over the valley of the **river Allen** for a fine view of the mysterious ruined church standing in the middle of the **Knowlton Circles**. The **Circles** are a Neolithic henge monument and it is fascinating to discover a Christian church in their midst! When you come to a junction of several paths keep straight ahead, with a hedge on your right and an open field on your left. The path continues through a wood to a crosstrack. Bear right for a few yards, then turn left through a gate to resume your former heading towards a farm. Go through a gate, cross the approach to the farm and cross a stile to a road.

⑤ Turn right downhill to a road junction in **Wimborne St Giles** just before **Bull Bridge**. Our route is left here, towards **Monkton Up Wimborne**, but before doing so you

THE DROVERS' INN AT GUSSAGE ALL SAINTS

could turn right and explore **Wimborne St Giles village**.

You pass the large, 17th-century mill house on your left and on the other side of the road the weathered remains of the village stocks. Beyond the green stands an impressive row of almshouses built in 1624 and adjoining them a fine church. The interior was badly damaged by fire in 1908 and was rebuilt in a richly decorated style by the distinguished architect Sir Ninian Comper. There is a splendid series of Shaftesbury memorials which include one to the famous humanitarian seventh Earl (in the family pew). His main memorial is Eros in London's Piccadilly Circus; his arrow is aligned with Wimborne St Giles. St Giles House, their family home since the 15th century, is hidden among the trees.

⑥ After visiting the village follow the road signed for **Monkton Up Wimborne**, past the **Bull Inn** on your left, for about 3/4 mile – as far as a sharp right bend.

⑦ Leave the road and keep straight on up the former coach road, following the bridleway sign to **Harley Gap**. The track climbs gently uphill through a wooded area – note the enormous yew trees! – to a crosstrack.

⑧ Bear right for about 50yds then keep to the same track as it curves left to lead you across **Harley Down**. On your left a wooded cleft slopes down to the **Gussage valley**. After almost a mile the woods on your left swing round to border your track and you emerge onto a wide, embanked crossing track. Climb the bank ahead to enjoy a splendid view.

This is Ackling Dyke. It comes as no surprise that so many Roman roads survive today, often running beneath our modern highways. The Romans built to last. The earth from the ditches was heaped in the centre and large heavy stones were placed on top as a foundation. This was surfaced with a rammed layer of fine aggregate. Originally the road would have been about 40ft wide, room for ten legionaries to march abreast.

⑨ Turn left to follow **Ackling Dyke**, passing a turning into a field on the left, for about 3/4 mile to a post marked with blue bridleway signs on the left.

⑩ Leave the Roman road here and turn left beside a meadow with a hedge on your right. (Although not marked as such on the OS map this is a right of way.) The meadow has been 'set aside' and is full of wild flowers and butterflies in summer.

Over the meadow you come to **Burtt's Harley wood**. Follow the path as it winds beside the wood richly carpeted in spring with primroses, violets and anemones. After about $^{1}/_{4}$ mile the path swings right and becomes a wide grassy way leading gently downhill between hedges. Keep to the track as it curves left to continue downhill. As you near the foot of the hill follow the line of the hedge on the right and bear right a little uphill to meet a well-defined crossing track, **Harley Lane**.

⑪ Turn right along Harley Lane, which leads you down into **Gussage All Saints**, passing the church on the right.

The church stands in a commanding position on the hillside. Built almost entirely in the 14th century, the interior is high and well-lit with cusped arches inside the windows and an interesting 14th-century tomb with a carved canopy. The 18th-century organ once stood in Westminster Abbey.

⑫ You come to the War Memorial at the foot of the lane, where a nicely placed seat invites you to rest and enjoy a view across a bridge over the tiny **Gussage stream** to the downs rising beyond. Turn left to walk through the village, a charming mix of brick and cob houses with colourful gardens, to return to the **Drovers' Inn** on your left.

Date walk completed:

Walk 20

LONGHAM, CANFORD MAGNA AND THE RIVER STOUR

THE RIVER STOUR AT CANFORD MAGNA

Distance:
9 miles

Starting point:
Patrons can leave cars in either of the White Hart's car parks. There is one behind the pub and another opposite the pub on the other side of the road. GR 066985

Maps: OS Explorer 118 Shaftesbury and Cranborne Chase and Outdoor Leisure 22 New Forest

How to get there: *Longham is beside the A348 about 2 miles south-east of Wimborne Minster. Heading west along the A31, follow the signs for Poole along the A347, then continue down the A348 for Longham. Pass the church and the White Hart is on your right. Approaching from Wimborne Minster along the B3073, turn right at the church.*

Although so close to Bournemouth, most of this walk follows peaceful meadow paths close to the river Stour as it flows through the parkland surrounding Canford Manor. This impressive building, once the home of the Earls of Salisbury, became a public school in 1923, ending 80 years of residence by the family of Lord Wimborne. The old manor was enlarged in the mid-19th century in the fashionable Gothic style by Sir Charles Barry to include its most distinctive feature, the tall entrance tower. From the White Hart at Longham we follow the Stour Valley Way to one of the estate villages, Canford Magna, an attractive mix of old houses, more modern villas and elaborate Victorian cottages built to house the tenants on the estate. After crossing the Stour we enjoy a riverside ramble with splendid views of Canford Manor before following part of the Ferndown, Stour and Forest Trail to return to Longham.

The **White Hart** pub in Longham is over 400 years old. In the 18th century it was the headquarters of Isaac Gulliver, known as 'the gentle smuggler' as he claimed no Customs Officer was ever killed during encounters with his gang. Quick-witted and utterly fearless he led a small army of about 50 men organising runs of contraband goods from France, chiefly tea, spirits, tobacco and luxury goods. As you enter this welcoming pub it is easy to imagine Gulliver in some dark corner plotting his next run over a foaming jug of the White Hart's excellent ale! The atmosphere is that of a ship's cabin, with low beamed ceilings, deep window seats and wooden settles. And as is only proper in a pub so old there is a resident ghost, the mysterious 'Lady of Longham'. Fortunately she prefers the attic to the bar!

Here you can enjoy well-kept Badger ales and choose from a varied menu of excellent home-cooked dishes. Pies baked in the old-fashioned way with crusts top and bottom are popular, especially 'Desperate Dan' – a steak-and-kidney masterpiece. Ham is oven-roasted on the bone and a range of pan-fried meals are served with home-made sauces to suit your taste. Sweets include apple and blackberry pie and a light syrup sponge.

The pub is open *on Mondays and Tuesdays from 12 noon to 3 pm and from 5 pm to 11 pm. The rest of the week it is open all day from 12 noon to 11 pm. Meals are served from 12 noon to 2.30 pm and from 6.30 pm to 9 pm. Telephone: 01202 572326.*

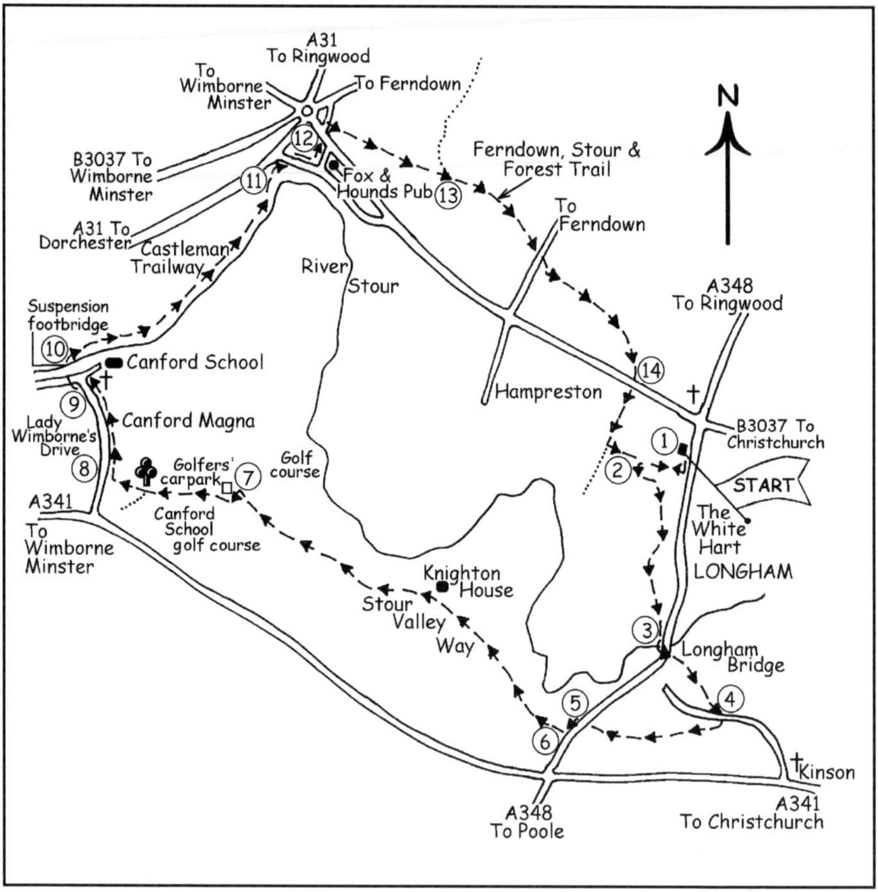

① Leave with the front of the **White Hart** on your right and walk along the grass beside the A348 for about 200 yards then turn right along **Green Lane**.

② After about 1/4 mile look carefully for a wooden railed entry on your left. Turn left and follow the fenced path beside embankments on your right. These surround former gravel pits which Bournemouth and West Hampshire Water Company are converting into lakes to store normally wasted winter rains from the **Stour**.

Keep to the fenced path as it twists and turns round the embankments. The path crosses a track and passes a bungalow on the left to bring you to a stile in front a field. Cross the stile and keep straight ahead, with a fence on your right, to a stile on your right. Cross this and bear left past the pumping station to meet the A348.

③ Turn right to cross **Longham Bridge** over the **Stour**. Just over the bridge turn left to follow a narrow gravel path signed for the **Stour Valley Way**. The path curves right away from the river with a stream on the left. Through the trees you will see the Norman tower of **Kinson church**, where Isaac Gulliver often concealed his contraband. Follow the path as it curves right to a lane.

④ Turn left along the lane for a few yards then turn right to continue along the **Stour Valley Way**. This

THE WHITE HART, LONGHAM, ONCE THE HEADQUARTERS OF THE 'GENTLE SMUGGLER'

very pleasant path runs beside a stream with trees on your right to bring you back to the A348.

⑤ Go through a gate and turn left beside the road for about 100yds to the sign for the **Stour Valley Way** across the road on your right.

⑥ Turn right following the direction of the sign through two gates. A faint path leads over the grass ahead just to the left of a pylon. The path becomes better defined as it leads through a gateway and continues beside a fence on the right. Go through another gate and keep ahead along the hedged track. Cross a stream and go through another gate. A tree-shaded path leads past **Knighton House**, dating from the 17th century with timber-framed cob and brick walls. Continue past a row of estate cottages on your left, along a wide, gravelled track to meet a lane. A golf course is on your right. Keep ahead along a narrow gravelled path to the right of the lane and continue to follow it when it switches to the left. When the gravel track curves left keep straight on beside the lane to a car park just before the lane bears right.

⑦ Turn left along the left hand edge of the car park. Cross a stile and follow the line of marked posts straight across **Canford School golf course**. (The second post is green and hard to spot – head towards a clump of trees.) Cross a gravel track and follow a narrow path into a wood. After a few yards the path divides. Take the right hand path which soon leaves the trees and continues, marked with posts, along the edge of a football field with a stream on your right. Go over a lane to the school and continue down the field to go through a gate to the road in **Canford Magna**.

⑧ Turn right to walk through the village. When the road curves left keep straight on downhill through the trees to pass the church on the right. Part of a Saxon church built in the middle of the 11th century has survived and forms the chancel of the present building.

⑨ Past the church a gatehouse on the right leads into **Canford School**. Bear left over the grass onto a surfaced track known as **Lady Wimborne's Drive**. This was constructed to enable the carriages of the Wimborne family to be driven easily to town. After a few yards turn right to cross the graceful suspension bridge over the **Stour**. Made of cast iron and steel it is the only one of its type in Dorset. The Guest family who lived at Canford in the 19th century were iron makers in South Wales and it seems likely that they had the bridge erected.

⑩ Bear right over the grass to walk beside the **Stour**, crossing stiles bearing the distinctive sign of the **Castleman Trailway**, a steam engine on a footprint. Follow the **Stour** for about 1¼ miles.

The Castleman Trailway is 16 miles long. Much of the way follows the route of the former Southampton to Dorchester railway line from Upton Country Park near Poole to the river Avon near Ringwood. It is named after Charles Castleman, who was chiefly responsible for building the line.

⑪ The path curves left to a track then bears right to cross a stile by some pine trees. Bear half-left across a field and go over a stile to the right of an underpass beneath the A31. Follow the sign for **Stapehill**, bearing right through a gateway and along a farm track to a lane. Turn left to follow the lane signed for **Stapehill**, passing the **Fox and Hounds** pub on your right, to meet the B3073.

⑫ Turn left for just a few yards then turn right into **Fox Lane**. Leave the **Castleman Trailway** here and turn almost immediately right, following a footpath sign, along a pleasant woodland track. Continue past a gate then beside meadows, crossing stiles and plank bridges.
A narrow path now tunnels through woodland before leading beside a tall deer fence on the left. A little stream is on your right. You walk through more woodland before following the fence again. Cross a final stile to a wide embanked crosstrack, part of the **Ferndown, Stour and Forest Trail**.

⑬ Turn right and keep to this pleasant track as it curves left to lead past an iron gate to a road. Cross straight over, go through another iron gate and follow the track ahead with open fields on your right. The track bears right through a wooded area to the B3073.

⑭ Cross the road and keep ahead down the track. Take the first turning on the left and continue along the track we followed at the beginning of the walk to rejoin the A348. Turn left to return to the **White Hart**.

Date walk completed: